LET IT BURN

BURN

Nika Michelle
&
Kenni York

Published in the United States of America

Cover Design: AMB Branding & Design

Chapter 1

Tyson

"Get down on the floor now and put your hands behind your fuckin' heads! This is a fuckin' robbery!" A loud, deep voice boomed behind me.

I immediately hit the floor as instructed. Not that I was the softest nigga in Atlanta, but I wasn't "bout that life". All I wanted to do was deposit my paycheck into my bank account. At that moment I was pissed that my stupid ass job had stopped doing direct deposit.

At first I was just flirting with the teller, I think her name was Ari. I'd seen her at the Bank of America on Panola Rd. in Lithonia, GA a few times. She was new and had just started working there a month or so ago. Usually she'd flirt back, but her supervisor was right beside her, so she kept it professional. I thought honey was sexy as hell.

Then boom, suddenly the place was getting robbed by some goon. Normally security would be there, but of course on the day that they weren't shit popped off. Damn, my black people. I shook my head because I could tell from the robber's voice that he was indeed an African American man, if I could even call him a man.

Of course I had no clue what was going on. It was so quiet at that point that you could hear a pin drop. I closed my eyes and actually prayed. Yeah, I prayed, which was something I knew that I needed to do more. I was twenty seven years old and my birthday was in a couple months. I wanted to make it.

'Lord, please let me get through this. I know that I'm not really a praying man. That's probably why this is happening. Forgive me for lying on my taxes for that extra stack. That was so greedy of me. Oh, and forgive me for mistreating my last girlfriend Crystal and every other woman that I hurt before her. I know that I'm the worst man in the world when it comes to relationships. Lord, I'll make up for all of my past transgressions...'

"Empty the drawers now! All of you! Hurry the fuck up before I start shooting motherfuckers! Don't do nothing stupid, 'cause I ain't got a goddamn thing to lose up in this bitch! If you hit the alarm everybody's gonna die up in here! Gimme a ink bag and I'll blowin' this motherfucker up! I'm so fuckin' serious!" The gunman yelled.

All I could do was wait it out. It wasn't like I could help the situation in any way. My heart was pounding and I could hear it because it was so loud. I was hoping that shit would be over soon so I could get home in one piece. The sound of gunshots made me cringe. Did somebody get killed?

"Motherfucker! I told that bitch not to try to push the fuckin' alarm!"

Oh shit! I wondered if he was referring to Ari. There was only one other female teller working that day. A few seconds later I heard the sound of sirens.

After that I didn't even want to look up to see what was going on. It was suddenly quiet and then after what felt like forever I heard someone say, "DeKalb County Police Department is here. You can all get up now. It's safe."

I finally stood up on my feet glad to know that it was finally over. My eyes scanned the faces behind the glass and spotted Ari standing there with a stunned look on her pretty face. My guess was that the robber had used a very high caliber weapon to shatter the supposedly bullet proof glass. Something inside of me made me want to comfort her, but at that point I didn't know what I could or could not do.

"Are you okay sir?" A female officer asked me. She was tall and slim built with long curly hair that was pulled up into a ponytail. Her caramel complexion was flawless and free of makeup.

"Uh huh, I'm fine." My eyes scanned the room because I didn't see the other female teller.

Then I saw the stretcher being wheeled out of the bank. The paramedics were working frantically to save her life. All I could do was shake my head at the thought of that being me…or Ari. I mean, I wasn't glad that it was her or anything. I was just thankful that no one else had been shot.

"I'm Officer Collins. Can I ask you a few questions?"

"Uh, yes." My nerves were still rattled, but I knew the routine. They had to clear everybody who was in the bank.

"Did you get a good look at the assailant?" She asked.

"No, I uh, I was depositing my check and he came up from behind and told us all to get down. I wasn't trying to look at him at that point," I explained.

She nodded and wrote something down in her little notepad.

"Okay. Uh, do you come inside of this bank often?"

I gave her a confused look. "What does that have to do with anything? I have an account here and I was simply trying to deposit my paycheck. This is the closest Bank of America on my way home from work. I don't have any more information for you. I just want to leave."

When I glanced up I saw Ari talking to a white, male officer. I really wanted to make sure that she was okay. If anything I was hoping she'd feel some type of way and finally give me her number. I wasn't trying to take advantage of her in a vulnerable state, but now was a better time than any. As far as women were concerned, I was ready to redeem myself. What had happened had me thinking about how short life was. Shit, I could've been killed, so something told me to go for it despite the circumstances.

After Officer Collins was finished questioning me, I noticed that Ari was talking to a coworker instead of the male cop. I figured he was done with his interrogation of her as well and she'd been cleared. Maybe she would be further questioned, because employees were often involved. They may have been suspicious about it being an inside job.

Cautiously, I made my way over to Ari and the woman that she was talking to. I assumed that she was a manager or something because I'd never seen her behind the glass working as a teller. As a matter of fact I'd never seen the older woman before. She was tall and slim with a short, natural hair style. Her almond complexion was smooth and wrinkle free, which further proved that black didn't crack.

Ari was so naturally beautiful. She stood about 5'7 and was voluptuously curvaceous with smooth mocha toned skin, light colored, exotic eyes, perfectly shaped lips and a cute little nose. Her shoulder length hair was styled to perfection every time I saw her. Not only that, but her lashes and brows were always on point and as a man I appreciated that. She also had the smile of an angel and her straight, white teeth proved that she'd probably worn braces as a kid.

"Uh, excuse me," I said politely to the two women as they spoke in hushed tones. "I just wanted to make sure that you were okay Ari."

She peered up at me with tear stained cheeks. "I'm fine. It's just…well, Kelly didn't make it."

The older woman looked up at me. "Are you okay young man?"

"Yes, I am. I'm so sorry. How about you?"

She nodded and forced a smile on her face.

"Considering the circumstances, I'll be okay I guess. I just hate that happened to Kelly. She just had a baby three months ago and got married last year." Her voice cracked and Ari grabbed her hand.

"I'm sorry to interrupt. I just wanted to make sure that you were okay." I quickly realized that it wasn't the time to get her number because the other woman wasn't budging.

"Camille, can you please come to the back for a minute?" Another bank employee asked as he approached.

"Sure," the older woman excused herself and Ari and I were finally alone.

"I don't want to come off wrong, but I've been wanting your number for a long time. I know that this may not be the best timing, but after what happened, I figured why not ask." I had to get it out before I lost my courage.

"I was waiting for you to ask. It's 404…"

"Hold on beautiful. Let me get to my contacts." I pressed the necessary icon on my phone as my heart beat increased again. "Okay, go ahead."

* * *

When I got home I was hoping to relax and grab a beer after what had happened at the bank, but that thought was too good to be true. My ex-girlfriend Lauryn's car was in my drive way, which immediately made my heart drop. We'd been together for about a year before she got pregnant. Being the stand-up guy that my parents raised, I asked her to marry me. When the baby came out looking biracial I tripped.

Shit, I was dark as night, 6'1, with wavy hair that I kept cut close. My eyes were also dark and slanted. Women often compared me to the model Tyson, which was very coincidental. Like him I also had roots in Jamaica. My father Jason Reid was born there, but had migrated to Atlanta with his parents when he was five. My mother, Tyra Reid was a dark skinned beauty from New Orleans who had moved to Atlanta when she was nineteen. She had met my father a year later and they'd been together ever since.

Lauryn was also a dark complexioned woman, so I questioned her faithfulness. It wasn't possible for us two to produce a baby that was damn near white. True, I wasn't the most faithful man, but I hadn't made any babies on her ass. A DNA test proved that the little boy wasn't mine and I broke it off with her. She later confessed that she had slept with my neighbor, who was a white man. I moved away from that spot because I wanted to kill old dude. That was over a year ago and despite that fucked up shit, she didn't seem to want to let go.

I had eventually moved on with Crystal, who I had treated like shit as a result of what Lauryn had done to me. Of course my behavior and Lauryn's jealousy drove her away. I'd been single now for six months.

"What do you want Lauryn?" I asked once I made it to her.

She was leaning against the red Honda Accord that she had bought from the dealership I worked at. Yes, I was a car salesman and a good one at that. That was how we had met.

"I want you back Ty. I fucked up. I admit that and I've been trying to make it up to you ever since. Tyson Jr. needs a father and…"

I couldn't help but laugh at her dumb ass. "What the fuck does that have to do with me? That's your problem. Last time I checked he has a father, so you need to be stalking him. Not me."

She sucked her teeth in annoyance and followed me as I made my way toward the front door. I turned around and faced her as I walked backwards.

"I love you Ty and I won't give up until…"

"I'm gonna get a restraining order against your crazy ass!" As I turned around I felt a crushing blow to the side of my head.

I grabbed her hand swiftly and noticed that she was holding a huge rock.

Suddenly I felt light headed and dizzy as hell.

"What the fuck?" I asked her weakly as two of her stood in front of me. Was I seeing double?

Then all I saw was black.

* * *

"You okay? Can you hear me?" The voice sounded distant at first and then closer.

My eyes fluttered open, but my vision was still blurry. The direct glare of the sun was definitely not helping me focus on the person in front of me.

"Yes," I whispered feeling the throbbing pain in my head.

Then I remembered.

"She hit me in the head with a rock...Lauryn..."

"Who hit you with a rock?" The voice was feminine and I realized when her face finally came into focus that it was my neighbor Mrs. Jennings. "The young lady who drove off in the red car?"

She was a nosy old lady whose husband had died from cancer a few years ago. Her family didn't come around much, so she relied on the community gossip to keep her going. I kind of liked that she minded everybody else's business. That way I knew that she'd always see what was going on.

"Yes."

"It's gonna be alright. The ambulance is on the way. I saw you laid out here with blood coming from your head, so I didn't know what happened. You wasn't responding so I called 911. Tell the police everything." She was a short, stout brown skinned woman with short, salt and pepper curls.

"Thank you Mrs. Jennings," I said gratefully.

"You're most welcome and call me Nancy."

* * *

"Mr. Reid, you have suffered a minor concussion due to the fall on the concrete that resulted after the initial blow to your head. You are okay for release now. Your tests show normal brain activity. Right now you'll just have to take it easy and manage the pain. Here are your discharge papers as well as your prescription for pain meds and antibiotic cream for the abrasions," the young nurse explained as she passed me the proper documents.

"Thank you very much. I guess I'll be on with my day," I said as my thoughts drifted.

First a bank robbery and then a damn concussion courtesy of a crazy ass bitch from my past. What a fucking day. I shook my head as I stood up from the exam bed. The police had been called and I gave them a report of what had happened. Hell yeah I was going to press charges. How the hell did Lauryn have the audacity to show up at my house to attack me if I didn't agree to be with her? It had to have been planned because she already had the rock in her hand. I wondered what the hell had kept her from killing me and I wasn't going to wait to let her finish me off.

When I got to my car I pulled out my cell phone to call Ari. After the chaotic day

I'd had, I needed someone to talk to. I just hoped she'd be available.

After three rings I heard her soft, sweet voice.

"Hello."

"Hey Ari. This is Tyson, from the bank."

I could hear the smile in her voice. "I know. How are you considering the day we had?"

"Hmm, that's not even half of it. You wouldn't believe what happened when I got home."

Chapter 2

Ari

I smiled at my reflection in the mirror as his voice crooned in my ear. Hearing about the series of unfortunate events that constituted his day was very believable to me. Especially considering that I was there during the bank robbery. I felt bad about what happened to Kelly, but I had to remind myself that things like that happened. Sometimes innocent people got hurt when random things like bank robberies went down. I was grateful that shit didn't go all the way left and that I didn't get hurt in any way. I was absolutely blessed.

The shine of my perfectly crowned, dazzling white teeth greeted me as I reveled in my own beauty. I was blessed in other ways as well. I knew that I turned heads whenever I entered a room. My round figure, pretty smooth brown skin, and inviting lips made men –and some women – drool at the proposition of getting a taste of me or at least a bit of my attention. I wasn't narcissistic, it was just that I knew where I'd come from and I knew what I was working with. Shit, I had paid enough to ensure that everything was right and tight.

"All I need right now is a good drink and some good company," Tyson was saying. "You have plans this evening?"

"Not at all," I told him. "You wanna meet up somewhere?"

"Yeah. What are you in the mood for?"

I was a simple chick and I figured that Tyson was a simple type of dude. No need in coming across as high-maintenance. "How about wings and drinks at the JR Crickets on Panola."

His hesitation was noticeable but seconds later he agreed. "Alright, that's cool. You wanna meet me there around 8:00? That'll give me time to get home and get cleaned up."

"Sounds good," I told him. "Looking forward to it. Then you can tell me about what other craziness your day has been tainted with."

"Bet. Okay, pretty lady. See you then."

I disconnected the call and headed to my closet to find which banging outfit I could piece together to make this man's eyes bulge out of his head. Tyson was a cutie. He had that sex appeal that made a woman's panties wet immediately. I wondered how many hearts he'd broken over his lifetime and how many times he'd had his broken. I wanted him to be into me. I wanted him to lust for me and grow attached to me. I wanted him to get caught up in me and see how perfectly our lives could be blended together. The way I saw it, we looked good together. Him with his fine, strong masculine features and his lucrative career as a car salesman. Oh yeah, I knew what his income was looking like after all of the deposits I'd made for him over the last month and a half. You could learn a lot about a dude by the way his portfolio looked. From the zeros resting in the savings account he held with Bank of America, I knew that he was responsible. He wasn't shitting away his money, but was holding on to his coins. Judging by the moderate amount of funds in his primary checking account and the fact that the withdrawals listed were typically from utility companies, I knew that he was not only responsible, but that he was also organized. A second checking account was present for what appeared to be his fun, recreational purchases. I also knew that the man was preparing for a future. This was made plain by the mortgage account he had with my bank. No man was forking over mortgage payments if he wasn't preparing for a family. Who knew? Maybe Tyson would see me as the woman with whom to build said family.

I settled upon a pair of tight, form fitting dark denim skinny jeans and a sheer white blouse. I knew that Tyson's eyes would never leave the vision of my plump, juicy breasts pushed up with my Victoria's Secrets navy blue push up bra as if my girls really needed the extra experience. My height increased to an impressive 6'3 due to my six inch heels. I'm not exactly a midget, but there was something men went crazy about when a chick put on heels. Honestly, I couldn't think of anything sexier than a woman sashaying around with her curves twitching seductively. A confidence like no other exuded when a woman was comfortable in a pair of cute heels.

All ready to go with my lips popping and my outfit doing its thing, I left out of my sleek condo in the heart of Stone Mountain, slipped into my white MKZ and headed towards J.R. Crickets. I'd chosen the spot because of its location. Not only was it down the street from my job, but it was in a general area that I felt a sense of familiarity with. After a twenty minute drive I was sitting inside of the tiny, nearly crowded wing spot when Tyson sauntered into the building with his stunna shades on. He shot me a cocky smile and I sipped on my Midoria Sour through the thin black straw sticking out of my glass. My eyes twinkled as I blushed while he headed to our table.

"Beautiful as always," Tyson said as he hugged me from my seated position.

I inhaled slightly and took in the strong scent of his Gucci cologne. My eyes fluttered and I damn near wanted to bite into his neck before he broke our embrace. I pulled it together quickly as he took his seat and removed his shades.

"Hot date?" I asked jokingly as I surveyed his swag.

"Yeah, with the most stunning woman in all of Metro Atlanta."

Good answer, I thought as I took another sip of my cocktail.

"What you drinking on?"

"A Midori Sour," I told him. "I would have ordered something for you, but I wasn't sure if you were more of a Heineken man, or an E&J type of dude."

"Honestly, you can't go wrong with either one," he replied. "Look at you. Already knowing a brother." He flagged down a waitress and ordered an E&J with Coke while I remained silent.

"Should I put your orders in now as well or do you need a minute?" The tatted up waitress asked.

"You know what you want?" Tyson asked me as he poured over the menu.

I shrugged. "I'm flexible. Order whatever and we can share it. I'm not picky."

Tyson smiled and I knew that he was digging being out with me already. "Lemme get the thirty piece sweet and spicy wings with a large fry."

The waitress took our menus and excused herself to go put in our orders. I took the time to study Tyson's face and couldn't help but notice his pained expression and a tiny knot on the left side of his head.

"So tell me about the craziness that consumed the rest of your day," I inquired.

"Mannnnn," he sang as he leaned back in his chair and looked at me. "It's like

I'm a lightning bolt for random crazy events today. So I get home after leaving the bank and my ex-girlfriend is posted up in my driveway. Already I know she's about to be on some other shit that I'm not really in the mood for."

"You broke up on bad terms?"

"Bad terms is an understatement. We broke up on catastrophic terms. This chick gets pregnant and tries to pass the kid off as mine, right? Baby comes out all kinds of light bright. I mean, there's no way possible that child came from my seed. Then she goes and names the baby after me knowing full well that she was messing around with my white neighbor."

"Your white neighbor?" I asked in shock. "Shut up! How do you manage to still live next door to that man knowing that he was creeping with your girlfriend? You sure she wasn't over there to see him?" I was trying to make light of the situation, but the lines of fury covering his forehead made it clear to me that this was not funny at all to Tyson.

"Naw, I moved from there. I had to get away from that area, from that dude, and I thought I was getting away from her trifling ass but she's like a stalker, man. Done tracked me down, popping over to my spot ever so often." He paused when the waitress brought over his drink and didn't commence to speaking until after he'd taken a hearty gulp. "So yeah, she's at my place and starts going into her usual song and dance about how she messed up, how she wanted to get back with me, and how the baby –she calls him Tyson Jr – needs his daddy."

I was galled at the thought. "Is she for real? I hope you told her to go find Opie and tell his ass to parent the little milky baby."

Tyson laughed at my apparent disdain for his crazy ex-girlfriend and her antics.

"You know I did. I was trying to be tactful and tell her to get the hell on but this nut practically follows me to my front door and clocks me with a fuckin' rock."

I gasped and stared at him in disbelief. "Psycho bitch! Are you okay?" I looked him over a little harder now, searching for any signs that he was badly hurt after being accosted.

Tyson took another gulp of his drink. "I'm good. I was bleeding some and my neighbor Mrs. Jennings came out to see about me. Man, a brother passed out and was laid the fuck out. Ambulance took to me to the hospital, but everything's good. Slight swelling, no apparent brain injury."

My hand covered my chest as if stopping my heart from jumping out of it. "But still. That had the potential to go very wrong."

"Yeah it did," he agreed.

"Just like at the bank today."

Tyson shook his head. "Sorry again about your coworker. That was a real unfortunate situation. These dudes don't be thinking out here in these streets. So much other stuff they could be doing with their lives. Being successful and productive, you know?"

"Like you," I stated.

Our eyes met.

Tyson gave a half smile. "I guess so."

"No shame in it. I can tell you're a good guy, Tyson Reid. That's why the crazy none-baby-mama's trying her best to hold on to you."

"Hmmm. Well, I can tell you're a pretty awesome woman yourself, Ms. Ari…" he was at a loss for my last name since it wasn't present on my ID badge at work.

"Smit," I filled in for him.

"Ms. Ari Smit."

I could tell that he was taken aback by my last name. It wasn't very common, but that was something that I prided myself in – being different. My cell rang before either of us had the opportunity to say anything. I pulled it from my purse, looked at the CALLER ID, and nonchalantly sent the

caller to voicemail. It was someone that
could wait.

"So, yeah," I said. "That nut needs to
be arrested for going around hitting folks
with rocks. That's just crazy."

"Trust me, I'll be getting a restraining
order soon enough."

"And to think that she was a
girlfriend. I mean, I'm assuming you
actually loved her at some point."

Tyson shook his head in disgust. "I
did. I don't see why or how now though."

"Well, let's be glad that the baby
wasn't yours honey and that all she did leave
you with was a slightly swollen lump on
your skull and nothing fatal that you can't
get rid of." I gave him a knowing look and
picked up my drink.

Tyson shuddered. "Thank God!" He sounded completely grateful for the Lord's mercy in that moment.

"Here you go," the waitress said as she returned to the table with our wings. "Can I get you something else?"

"Nope, we're good," Tyson told her. As the woman walked away, Tyson looked over at me and reached for my hand. "You mind if we pray over the food?"

I sat my glass down and quickly took his hand. I tingled a bit on the inside, impressed with the way he'd presented himself. Mentally, I added 'Christian' to my list of his character traits. Yes, I was assessing Tyson from all angles and from the looks of things he was seemingly Mr. Perfect. I bowed my head and remained silent while harboring my own thoughts as he said the grace. Once he uttered the word 'amen' I lingered a second too long before releasing his hand.

"I have a good feeling about you," Tyson said as our fingers slowly parted ways.

"Is that so?"

"It is indeed. I get the feeling that you're going to change my life."

I simply smiled. Tyson Reid had no idea.

Chapter 3

Tyson

Almost three weeks had passed and Ari and I were inseparable. To be honest in such a short time, I couldn't imagine going too long without seeing her, or at least hearing her voice. I was smitten by her and like a lady, she was making me wait for it. It was a good thing Lauryn hadn't been around since her attack on me because I'd hate for her to bump heads with Ari.

Ari carried herself like a lady, but she seemed to be able to hold her own. Still, I didn't want to put her in a fucked up position. That was why I had taken the proper steps to get a restraining order in place. I'd also pressed charges on Lauryn for assault. At that point she hadn't been arrested because the police couldn't locate

her. My guess was her psycho ass was
hiding out somewhere.

She was originally from Macon, so I
figured that she was hiding out there with
family members. I couldn't fathom why
she'd attack me like that. It was so odd.
She'd always been emotionally unstable, but
never violent. I guess you never really knew
a person's capabilities when they were
feeling some type of way.

Ari and I had always met up
somewhere and over the past few weeks had
gone to dinner, bowling, dancing, bar
hopping, a few night clubs/lounges, the
movies and even a spa for massages.
Tonight I wanted us to have some real,
private time. So, I was cooking for her and
hoping to finally get some of that good
loving I knew she had. Damn, I was ready.

It was a shame for a woman to be that damn fine. Her body was so enticingly thick and when I held her close to me she felt so soft. A few times she had let my hands linger below her slim waist and caress that perfectly round ass. I couldn't wait to palm it like a basketball while I…

The sound of my phone ringing interrupted my nasty thoughts. When I looked down at the phone I noticed Ari's number. I dried my hands off on a towel and turned the sound of Usher's crooning all the way down.

"Hello gorgeous. How're you?" I asked probably sounding a little too anxious.

"I'm great and how are you handsome?" Her voice was so sweet and soothing to my ears. I could get used to listening to her.

That woman was the epitome of feminine perfection. Not only was she pleasing to the eyes, but she was not one of those loud, nagging chicks. Instead she had a way of getting her point across in a very easy going way. I guess you could say that she was assertive instead of aggressive and she had a great sense of humor.

"Even better now that I hear your sexy voice. I hope you're callin' to tell me that you're on your way over." I turned the stove down to keep our Italian dinner of spaghetti and meatballs warm.

The garlic bread was inside of the convenient bread warmer and a fresh spinach salad was in the fridge. There was Chardonnay chilling on ice and the mood inside of my modernly furnished home was just right for romance. I'd even changed my sheets because I was hoping to get her fine ass between them. The Egyptian cotton sheets with a1500 thread count were only pulled out for special occasions, so I was hoping for some action.

"Yes, I'm like ten minutes away according to my GPS."

"Perfect."

"Well, I just wanted to let you know that I'll be there shortly."

"Cool."

We ended the call and my nerves were getting the best of me. What if she was one of those chicks who went by the ninety day rule? In that case would she be offended if I tried to take it there. I mean, we'd kissed, but it had never been anything hot and heavy. Her kisses were incredible though. All soft and sensual, but never really passionate. I was hoping to share some passion with her tonight.

At the sound of the doorbell ringing my heart raced. I didn't want to seem too anxious so I waited a few seconds before making my way to the door. I peeked out to be sure that it wasn't Lauryn's cray cray ass. It was the strikingly beautiful Ari, so I graciously opened the door.

She looked breathtaking in a long, low cut, form fitting white dress with a thigh high split on each side. Thighs and breasts were beckoning for my attention. Damn. Beautiful aqua colored peep toe high heels made her seem closer to my height. She also had on earrings, a bracelet and a necklace to match her shoes. Her makeup was light and natural looking and her hair was done up in bouncy spiral curls.

"Wow," I said breathlessly. "You look amazing."

She planted a soft peck on my lips before stepping inside.

"You're looking good too homey," she said with a smile as I closed the door behind her.

I was trying to change my status from homey to lover. If only she knew the things I'd do to her. Hmm, I pictured her thick ass thighs wrapped around my head as I licked and slurped on what I knew was one of the prettiest pussies I'd ever seen in my life. My mouth watered at the thought.

"You okay?" She asked suddenly knocking me back into reality.

I cleared my throat. "Oh yeah. I'm good. I hope you're hungry because I threw down."

"Oh really, so not only are you handsome and responsible, but you can cook too. Dang, why aren't you married yet?" She asked teasingly. "Any secret addictions or mental illnesses that I need to know about?"

I laughed. "I'm not married because I haven't been so lucky when it comes to relationships. I told you about my ex who pinned her baby on me. Well, we were engaged. Of course that didn't work out. Unfortunately the woman that I dated after her had to deal with the bitter side of me. I was kind of blaming her for Lauryn's actions when she had nothing to do with them. Eventually we decided to call it quits. No addictions or mental illnesses, but I might hit a joint or take a drink every once and a while." I didn't want to scare her off by adding that I'd never really been good to any of my girlfriends.

Not only was I not a faithful man, but I'd never put my all into a relationship before or after Lauryn. For some reason I wanted to try something different now. Ari made me want to actually give a real relationship a try. I wasn't getting any younger, so it was about time that I got serious about somebody.

Although I wanted to take her to my room and do all types of freaky shit to her, I also wanted to make her my woman. She seemed to have her head on straight and I had a feeling that I'd be going to sleep with a hard on. So, I decided to just let things flow. If she wanted to give me some, she would. I wasn't going to press the issue.

"Well, that's how it is sometimes. As long as you take something from each relationship. Like they say, some people are in your life only for a season. I truly believe that. We learn a lesson from that person and then we move on."

"Right," I agreed as I grabbed her hand and led her into the dining room.

"Oh, it smells delicious in here," she said as she took a look around.

The brown and black Italian marble counters and mahogany cabinets gave the room a rich, earthy look. There were all stainless steel appliances and state of the art décor. I took pride in my kitchen, which was a trait from having a southern mother who loved to cook. My father usually barbequed, but he could hold his own in the kitchen too. That was why I learned how to cook. There were no gender roles in my household. I had a younger sister and an older brother named Tyonna and Tyrone and we all did the same chores. Tyonna lived in Miami Florida and Tyrone lived in Texas. They were both married and so the pressure was on me to find a wife. Shit, I was working on it.

"Thank you. Why don't you have a seat, baby. I got this right here."

As I fixed our plates she got comfortable and sparked small talk. "So, who taught you how to cook?"

"I'm really close to my parents and they both know their way around the kitchen. I learned that women are not the only ones who should know how to cook. A man has to eat too, especially if he's single. Speaking of single. Why's a beautiful, intelligent woman like you not spoken for?

I'm so curious to know."

I poured some wine in her glass and
then placed her plate in front of her.

"Spaghetti, my favorite," she said
with a smile before taking a sip of wine.

"Chardonnay, also my favorite. I see that
you've been taking notes. A man who
listens. You continue to impress me Tyson."

I sat down across from her. "Yes, I do
listen, but you didn't answer my question
beautiful."

Her smile didn't fade, but something
in her eyes changed. "Well, I'm not married
because none of my relationships ever went
that way. I'm just glad I dodged an unhappy
marriage. I want to make sure that the right
man finds me, so I'm not bitter. I took what
I needed to take from my past and now I'm

the woman who stands before you. Even stronger and more beautiful than ever."

I raised my glass. "A toast to learning from the past. I know that I have. I've learned to never take advantage of a good thing. You should appreciate it, cherish it and make it yours forever. That's my plan."

We clicked our glasses together.

"Hmm," Ari said thoughtfully after she sipped her drink.

I wondered if I had come on too strong. "I'm sorry if…"

"Oh no," she cut me off quickly. "You don't have a reason to be sorry. I was just thinking about something. You didn't offend me at all."

"What were you thinking about?" I asked as I sprinkled Parmesan cheese on my spaghetti.

"How cute our kids would be." That beautiful, bright smile was on her face again.

I couldn't help but smile back. "Yes, we'd have gorgeous kids. Cute's an understatement."

She nodded in agreement.

"Uh, do you want some Parmesan cheese?"

"No, I'm good. Uh, I guess we should say grace."

"Yes, you go ahead this time." I didn't know if I wanted to be talking to God with the thoughts that were going through my head.

She said grace and I followed with a low "Amen."

We dug into the food and kept the conversation going. Of course, as always, I was enjoying how easy it was for us to talk. That was a sign that we'd be able to communicate. It had only been a few weeks though, so I didn't want to get beside myself.

"So, do you like to travel?" Ari asked after she swallowed her food.

I watched her sexy lips move as she talked. Damn, why the hell did she have to be so fine? That shit was making it so hard for me to focus.

"Oh yeah. I just don't really have time because I work so much. Gotta keep the bills paid so I can have something stacked up for retirement. Maybe then I can see the world. Hopefully I've found somebody to see it with." I kept my eyes on her and she didn't look away.

"A woman would be happy to go anywhere with you."

"I'm not really concerned about any woman other than you right now."

"Oh really?" She flashed those sexy dimples at me as she batted her eyelashes flirtatiously.

"Hell yeah. I'm so serious. Since the first time I saw you I wanted to get to know you. To be honest with you Ari, that's not like me at all. I'm the type of man who enjoys being a bachelor, but I've always been open to the possibility. I guess I was just waiting to meet the right one. To finally have that feeling that I'm feeling right now." My appetite for food was gone. I wanted to taste her.

She had finished a substantial amount of her food and that was a good sign. As she drank more of her wine, I could see her skin flush. Was she blushing?

"Did I say something wrong?"

She seemed to be so confident and in control, but I didn't want to offend her or make her nervous.

"No, just a little bit more turned on than I should be." She fanned herself playfully. "You're a very good looking man. To be honest, you're fucking hot."

"Hmm, speaking of hot. Did the temperature suddenly increase up in here? Let me go turn the air up? Did you feel that?" I asked as I stood.

"Umm, yeah. I think you should turn the air up."

"How's the food by the way?"

"Delicious. Can't you tell? My plate's almost completely clean. Handsome, smart, hard-working, a gentleman who can cook, the list just goes on and on and on. You have to be too good to be true."

She licked her lips sexily and all I could do was stand there and stare. When she cleared her throat I remembered that I was supposed to be going to turn the air up.

"You just wait and see. I got a lot more to show your pretty ass. Uh, let me go turn the air up. I'll be right back." I walked off to the thermostat and when I returned she was pouring more wine in her glass.

"Need more liquid courage?" I asked as I admired her ample backside.

She laughed as she spun around to face me. "No, I'm fine being completely sober since I actually really like you."

I closed the distance between us and then leaned over to kiss her sweet lips. They tasted slightly of Chardonnay and were just as intoxicating. After that I grabbed the glass from her hand and put it on the table. She wrapped her arms around my neck and got more into the kiss that time. Oh yeah, there was the passion. I was so damn hard at that point and I knew that she could feel it.

Suddenly without warning, Ari pulled away. She wiped the side of her mouth, and grabbed the wine glass. After draining it empty, she rubbed her hands on her dress nervously.

"I don't want to rush this Tyson. I mean, I'm not that type of…"

"I know. I'm sorry. I just…I won't lie. You're so damn gorgeous and my attraction to you is hella strong. I can't control how you make me feel and how my body reacts to you. You smell so good and you're driving me crazy right now. Shit, what is that fragrance, mami?" I had to know.

"Lotus Flower Bomb."

I couldn't help but let out a chuckle and then I pulled her into my body for an embrace.

"I won't rush you Ari," I whispered in her ear. "Something tells me that you're so worth waiting for."

That seductive ass smile decorated her beautiful face once again. My heart skipped a beat. "There is something I can do though," she said sexily.

My eyes widened curiously. "What's that?"

She gently pushed me against the wall before dropping down to her knees. When she peered up at me with those smoldering eyes, I was weak as hell. Was she about to do what I think she was about to do? Oh wow. That was even better than getting some pussy.

As she unbuckled my belt and then my pants all I could do was think about how good her hot mouth was going to feel wrapped around my hardness. It was going to be a relief to feel the wetness, and the suction. Oh, I hoped she was good at that shit. Then I questioned why she would give me some head first. Maybe that was her thing. I didn't know, but I wasn't going to refuse it.

"Ohhh, shit…" I whispered as I stared down at her pretty ass with her mouth full of dick.

My eight solid inches were down her throat in no time. Oh, she had the deep throat game on lock and my knees were so weak that I thought I was going to crumble to the floor.

"Damn...fuck Ari..." My ass cheeks were clenching and my toes were curling so tight that they were popping.

She was slurping all loud while giving me that sloppy head. As she literally devoured my dick whole, she used her hand to jack me off at the same time. Oh, she was too good at that shit. I could see myself being a fool over her after that. She already had my bank account numbers and at that point she could have all of my money.

I had to close my eyes. That woman was giving me the best damn head I'd ever received in my fucking life. Next thing I knew my seeds were spewing into her hot mouth and I was about to cry because that shit felt so fucking good.

When she stood up on her feet and licked her lips I knew that she had swallowed every single ounce. All I could do was shake my head, because I was speechless. Damnit, I was in love.

Chapter 4

Ari

I'd dodged a bullet the night before and the memory was still so very fresh in my head. As I checked my mail a hot flash took over my body. Images of Tyson's strong chest heaving through his shirt and the way his head hung back while I gave him the best head I'm sure he'd ever had in his life ran through my mind. Subconsciously, I licked my lips as I headed to the front door of my condo with my mail in hand. My body was most certainly reacting to the lust that Tyson evoked. I was proud of myself for making it through the entire evening without stripping my clothes off and offering my body to him right there at the dining room table. Although it took some will power and a little personal reminder of what my true intent was, I was very sure that Tyson was more than accustomed to women throwing themselves at him mercilessly and shamelessly. I couldn't be one of those women, not if I was going for longevity and I was definitely in it for the long haul.

Stepping out of my orange and white platform sandals as soon as I crossed the threshold into my home, I made my way over to the couch and surveyed my mail. The familiar name and address on the rectangular business envelope brought a smile to my face. Money had a way of doing that—making a person excited. I opened the envelope, checked the numbers, and once I was certain that it looked correct I stuck the envelope into my purse making a mental note to make a deposit the very next day. I rose from the couch in pursuit of the kitchen to pour myself a glass of wine when my cell phone began to ring. Thinking it was Tyson, I fished the phone out of my purse and scrunched up my nose the moment I caught the name and number on the CALLER ID.

"Hello," I answered unenthusiastically as I made my way into the kitchen.

"You've been a hard one to get in contact with," the voice on the other end said into my ear.

I poured up a glass Pink Moscato unfazed. "Am I?"

"I was hoping that you'd be up to visiting sometime soon. Or I can come to you. Whichever you're more comfortable with. I just...I need to see you."

My eyebrow rose. I'd been thinking about changing my number ever since I had the lack of vision to contact her upon my move just a few months ago. I'd had a weak moment during the wee hours of the morning after watching a replay of *The Imitation of Life* on Lifetime. Feeling unusually emotional, I'd dialed her up thinking that maybe a reconciliation was in order, but as time went on it was my natural reaction to be hesitant to disclose any real information about myself, my life, or my whereabouts. I wasn't ready for a reunion, but I didn't have the heart to be completely cruel about it either.

"I'm really busy with work these days," I stated, savoring the flavor of the wine. "I don't really have time for trips or company."

"I wouldn't be any bother," she said.
"I could come and just be useful. Cook you
dinner, clean up for you...maybe meet you
for lunch, but I won't be any trouble. I just
really need to talk to you. In person I mean."

I took a deep breath and headed down
the hall to my bedroom. The feel of the shag
carpeting massaged my toes as I moved
along. Entering my bedroom where
everything was white and pristine, I couldn't
imagine anyone invading my personal
space—even her. I had a thing about privacy
and being alone. It was a thing that worked
for me, keeping people outside of my circle.
If it was one thing that I'd learned over the
years it was that I should never let anyone
in—never let myself be vulnerable or
gullible enough to believe that anyone was
ever really looking out for me. I was that

chick who stayed on guard. My past taught me a lot.

"I can't commit to that right now, okay," I told her as I took a seat on the chaise lounge that sat right underneath my bedroom window. Peering out at the view I could see the beautiful picturesque landscape of Stone Mountain in the distance. "I'm sure you understand."

"It's been years, Ar—"

I cringed and interjected before she could finish the pronunciation of my name. I didn't want to hear her say it and I definitely didn't want to hear her begging me to be a better daughter.

"Look, I really have to go. I'll call you later in the week." I'm sure we both knew that it was a lie.

She hesitated before responding. "I don't mean to bother you. You know I don't, but the Lord only gives us limited time here on Earth. I just don't want to waste any more of it."

My other line beeped and I couldn't have been any more thankful. I peered down at the CALLER ID and once again was dismayed to see that it wasn't Tyson calling. I was purposely not hitting him up yet forcing him to come to me. I was serious about the chase and day by day I was roping him in more and more. Still, he hadn't called yet and I wasn't any more enthusiastic about receiving this call than I was about receiving the one from my whining mother.

"As much as I'd love to sit here and assure you that the rapture won't occur before we make amends, I really must go," I stated sarcastically. "I have another call."

"Yes, yes. Okay. I understand. Be sure to call me back, okay?"

"Mmmhmm. Will do. I really have to go now, okay? Talk to you later." I clicked over before she could have a chance to turn the waterworks on and profess her undying maternal love for me. "What is it?" I asked, answering the other line.

"I need the other half of my money that you owe me," the voice demanded.

I took another sip of my wine and continued to stare out of the window. 3,2,1, I counted backwards in my mind. It was a technique I'd picked up during counseling once to help me control my anger and frustration. I was afraid that I'd hit negative five by the time I was actually calm between

the two of these fuck-tards that had decided
today was the day to grate my nerves.

"I'm sure you remember our
arrangement," I finally answered. "Half
upfront, which I made good on, and the
remaining balance once you've done the last
task."

"Look, I'm in a bind okay. You said
you'd help me out on this and I'm not
getting the money I need from my kid's
father. It's really tough right now and I'm
about to lose my place if I don't come up
with the rest of the money that I owe my
landlord."

"What did you do with the money I
already paid you?" I asked the woman.

"I paid two months of back rent and
paid off my car loan. I didn't want those

fuckers repossessing my shit. I need to be able to get to school and work, you know?"

"Ren, Ren, Ren," I chanted, calling her by the nickname I'd donned her with. I shook my head. How had she gotten herself to this point? When I first met the chick she was desperate to do anything to keep herself afloat. Struggling to keep her kid clothed and fed while going to nursing school during the day and working at a nursing home at night. Her problem had started with falling in love with the wrong man who hadn't been very understanding of her attempts to remain independent. Short of the long, Ren was almost helpless with no man to help her, not that I felt a man was exactly what she needed. No, what she needed to do was grow some proverbial balls and woman the fuck up.

I'd taken mercy upon her during our chance meeting months ago and threw her some change to a few odd jobs for me in assistance of my transition to Atlanta. By 'some change' I mean a nice check for $5,000.00 with another $5,000.00 coming her way once she'd finished her to do list.

"Can you help me out with an advance or what?" Ren asked me.

"No," I said flat out, unmoved by the pathetic tone of her voice. "But we can get the ball rolling with the rest of your tasks so that you can get your payoff."

"What is the point of all this anyway?" she huffed. "I mean, you could just take care of this stuff yourself and leave me out of it. Why do I feel like I'm being set up or something?"

Sick of her tirade, the tone of my voice escalated. "Look around! Who else is helping you? I took pity on you when I coulda left you struggling to rub two pennies together. If I wanted to fuck with you or fuck you over don't you think I would just go ahead and do that? Think of everything you've been through Ren. Think about it. Now ask yourself, do you really think that I'm your enemy? Do you really think that I, the person putting cold cash in your pocket, am the one who's out to get you? If you wanna roll over and be a doormat, then fine. Be a doormat. Be weak, Ren. Forget the tasks and just try to figure your situation out on your own. Bye."

"No wait!" Her desperation wouldn't let the chance of getting that other five stacks out of her grasp. "Just wait! I wasn't accusing you of nothing. You did save my ass with the money…I'm just saying…what happens if—"

"You don't have time for doubts," I told her. "You have a kid to take care of and yourself. There's no room for doubts. Either you're in or you're not. What's it going to be?"

She sighed deeply and I could almost imagine her slumping to the floor with her face in her hands. "I'm in," she said almost reluctantly, a slave to the mighty dollar. "What's next?"

I smiled and tried to contain my giggle of triumph. It felt good to pull someone back up onto the ledge when they seemed to be so close to just dropping off into oblivion. "Sending you a text within the next couple of minutes. I need this taken care of within the next 24 hours."

"Okay. And after that?"

"Two more things after that sweet pea and then the $5,000.00 is all yours. Deal?"

"Deal."

"Check your text in a bit. Don't call me back when it's done. I'll call you." I disconnected the call and stared at my phone. Ren was right. Some of these things I could just do myself but I felt obligated to help her out. I considered it my humanitarian duty.

My fingers got busy typing out the errand that I needed her to attend to for me tomorrow, but before I could press send, the phone began to ring in my hand. I was apparently very popular this evening. This time it was the call I'd been waiting for.

This Negro had gone damn near the whole day without saying boo to me and I had half the mind to send his ass to voicemail and let him sweat a little bit. But, I was anxious to speak him so I pressed the TALK button, put on a smile, and gave a sweet and seductive salutation. "Hey you!"

"What's good, beautiful?" He asked sending shivers up and down my spine.

Each time this man called me beautiful it had the same effect on me. Something deep within my spirit was stoked about his rapidly growing affection for me. Hearing the apparent adoration in his voice made me giddy.

"I was just sitting here thinking about you," I said, stroking his ego.

"Yeah? What were you thinking?"

"That I miss you."

"Is that right?" I could hear the smile in his voice.

"Mmmhmm. And I was thinking about you and me maybe going out tomorrow night."

"What did you have in mind?"

"I have tickets…" I purposely let my voice trail off to entice him.

"To what?" He asked cautiously. "Some ballet or something? Some male-bashing play with a dude wearing a dress? Awww man, don't tell me that's where we are now. I wine and dine you, now I gotta go sit through some chick flick type of event to prove my love," he joked.

"Prove your love huh?" I repeated, wondering if he was already at the place where I was aiming to get him. "Relax, you male chauvinist pig," I said playfully to not give him any indication that I'd honestly read much into his last statement. "It's tickets to a Hawks game. But, if you don't wanna go I can just give them to my coworker and her husband."

"What!" He gushed. "Yo! I wanted to get season tickets this year but had to forgo 'em since I had to move into my new place and wanted to watch my funds. Girl, you're gon' make a grown man cry. I'm a Hawks fan, baby! All day, every day."

I smiled to myself and mentally patted myself on the back. "So, it's a date then?" I asked him. "Meet me at Phipps Arena tomorrow evening at 6:30? Game starts at 7:30."

"Hell yeah! I'll be there, beautiful. Thanks for inviting me. Which reminds me…there was something I wanted to invite you to as well."

My interest was piqued. "Oh?"

"Yeah. My ten year class reunion is coming up in the next month and I need to send an RSVP. It's a formal event. I was wondering if you'd like to go with me. I'd be the envy of every man in the room with you on my arm."

I bit my lip in contemplation. The thought of a large group of people prying into when and how we met and scrutinizing me from head to toe didn't sound too appealing to me. As confident as I was about my physique, I wasn't sure I wanted to be used as Tyson's trophy for the night. "Ten years huh?" I asked mindlessly as I envisioned the plethora of his exes surrounding us with questions about our relationship. Chicks could get really bitchy when they were jealous.

"Yeah. I know it's probably kinda early for formal events and stuff, so if you're not down it's cool. No pressure. But, I'd really like it if you'd accompany me Ari. In fact, I'd be honored."

"Well, in that case it would be my pleasure to be your date to your reunion," I said although a cutting feeling sunk into my gut. I ignored it and forged on. I was making progress and didn't want to regress by coming across as disinterested.

"Damn, my girlfriend is like superwoman. You're perfect Ari. Simply perfect. Thank you so much. I've never had a woman that's been so cooperative and so chill. I mean, you really go with the flow. I appreciate that. I really like that about you."

"Hmmm. Tell me something. When did I become your girlfriend sir?"

"The moment our eyes first met at your job...something told me that you were special...there was just something about you...something that drew me to you. It was almost...umm..."

"Kismet," I finished for him. "Yeah, I know the feeling Ty. I know it all too well." Silence filled the phone line for just a second. "Okay sir. I'll see you tomorrow evening."

"Tomorrow evening, beautiful."

I pressed the END button on my phone and returned to my text. Reading over it I quickly pressed the send button. I was looking forward to an exciting day tomorrow. First, I'd deposit my check into my credit union account, muddle through an easy day at work, and then see what the evening had in store…oh yeah, I was pretty sure that the Hawks game would be interesting too.

Chapter 5

Tyson

"Damn man, that chick got your nose wide open," my co-worker Donovan said with a wide grin.

He was also a salesman, but his numbers didn't look as good as mine. To say that I was worth more on paper was the way to describe it. I must admit, that I had more going on in the looks department too.

Don was tall and lanky with pecan brown skin. He was in his early thirties and resembled the rapper Jay-Z with his oversized facial features. It seemed off balance because he was such a small framed man. He was married to an average looking woman named Brandy, but he liked to trick off with younger chicks. They were obviously using him for his money. Not only was he not attractive, but he was also an asshole.

"Why you say that?" I asked taking a sip of water from a bottle of Aquafina.

"Cause you haven't even looked at that fine young thang over there." He gestured in the direction of who he was talking about with a nod of his head to not make it obvious.

My eyes followed and I had to agree. Honey was sexy as hell. Not only was she pretty, but her body was banging like a sub-woofer. She had ass for days and titties that were spilling out of her too small top. Still, I wasn't impressed. It was all probably fake. She was definitely no Ari. Of course I'd told Don about my new woman and he had to clown.

"She a'ight," I said nonchalantly.

Don shook his head in amazement. "Are you serious? You need glasses man. She is way more than a'ight."

I shrugged my shoulders. "If you say so."

Karl, who was showing her a white Lexus, glanced over in our direction and made a face behind old girl's back. I was sure that meant he was mesmerized by her beauty and booty too. When Karl pretended to be slapping her ass, Don broke out into hysterical laughter.

The chick turned around and Karl immediately pretended to be professional again. Those fools were stupid and childish. At that moment I wondered if I had been so obnoxious and disrespectful towards woman. I came to the conclusion that I was just like them, but something had changed.

After meeting Ari, I didn't really notice other women like I used to. Was I really starting to fall for her? Shit, I had to be. I wasn't myself lately and Don called me out on it.

"Wow man. It's official. Your ass is gone, straight up." He shook his head at me in disgust and walked away.

What the hell? I didn't know why he was saying that like it was such a bad thing. If he had a woman who looked like Ari he would understand how I felt. Not only was she bad as hell, but she was actually cool and intelligent. Qualities other than looks mattered, but I needed a woman to compliment my swag.

A few hours later I'd met my goal for the day relishing in the zeros that were going to be on my commission check. Damn, it was so easy to manipulate people into doing what I wanted them to do. At that moment I realized that I used the same tactics on women that I used to sell a car.

I shook my head in shame at how clueless I'd been. When I looked back on my relationship with Lauryn, I had probably driven her into my neighbor's arms. Not only was I neglectful to her after a while, but I was also not affectionate. She didn't get complimented, nor did I show her that I loved her. I mean, to get her I did all of that, but once she was mine, it stopped. Somewhere down the line I'd lost interest and I started fucking around with other women. What I should've done was be honest with her instead of stringing her along. Maybe I deserved her cheating on me and that rock to my dome.

As I made my way to my car my heart leaped in excitement. It was only three thirty, but I was looking forward to the Hawks game. I was born and raised in the A, so of course I had been a die-hard fan since I was a kid. I could remember the first time my dad took me to a game. I was six years old and he had good seats. My older brother was with us and it was like a dream come true. After that all I wanted to do was hoop. Shit, in high school I was the star point guard, because of that day.

Instead of calling Ari and seeming all pressed, I decided to wait until I was on my way to the arena. I was about to get swagged out. My brand new True Religion outfit was laid across my bed with a pair of J's to match. I'd even gone to Macy's for some new boxers. Something told me that I was getting some tonight.

* * *

When I got to the crib I made a mental note to make a call to the police to check on them issuing Lauryn the warrant and restraining order. I was tired of looking over my shoulders and shit. I'd even thought about moving, but I was buying my house, not renting. It wasn't that easy. Besides, I loved my spot.

After peeling off my work clothes I threw on a pair of black basketball shorts and a white gall shirt, or wife beater as most called it. Then I plopped down on the sofa and made a call to DeKalb County Police.

After the greeting I went right into it. "Yes, I'm calling to follow up with you about a warrant and protective order that I filed against someone. As far as I know they have not been officially served yet, because she hasn't been located. What is the status with that?"

"Can I please get your name sir?"

"Uh, yes. Tyson Reid, spelled R-E-I-D."

I could hear her clicking away on her computer.

"Okay sir, did you recently file for the order?" She asked sounding extra bored with her job.

"Yes, it was almost a month ago and due to the circumstances it was acted on right away. I was actually assaulted by the person I filed against." My impatience was growing. How many Tyson Reids were in her damn computer?

"Okay, here we are. Is the person the order is filed against named Lauryn Montgomery?"

I sighed in relief hoping that she would say that the order and warrant had been served.

"Yes, that's her."

"I'm sorry sir. The warrant nor order has been served. The assailant still hasn't been apprehended. According to our records an attempt was made earlier today at her address, but there has been no contact."

My impatience was turning into anger. "Are you serious? I already told them to check out the address that I gave them in Macon. What, am I supposed to wait for the bitch to kill me or something? Now I bet if I whoop her ass y'all would lock my black ass up!"

"Calm down sir. I understand your frustration, but we don't have the jurisdiction to serve a warrant in Macon. Now I can be sure that the authorities in Macon are aware of the warrant and execute it themselves."

"Why hasn't that been done already?" I really wanted to know.

"It may have been done already sir. Please hold while I get that information for you."

I let out a heavy sigh. "Okay."

Suddenly some elevator music started playing in my ear. I was pissed. There was no way that I was going to let that woman mess up my mood. I was ready to chill with my lady at the Hawks game, but the thought of Lauryn following us and causing a scene had crossed my mind. Damn I hoped that she was really in Macon. So far Ari hadn't been exposed to my drama and I didn't want her to be. I was really feeling her and I wasn't going to let my crazy ex jeopardize what we were building.

"Thank you so much for holding Mr. Reid. I was told that the warrant will be issued to the address that you provided first thing in the morning."

I pulled the phone away from my ear and just stared at it in disbelief. When I put it back to my ear I wasn't any calmer than I was at first.

"The morning? Oh wow. It's only four pm, so why can't it be served today?"

"I apologize Mr. Reid, but it's a procedure when you're transferring a warrant to another jurisdiction. I know that it's hard, but you have to trust the process. Is there anything else I can do for you today sir?"

I could tell that she was trying to get me off the damn phone and that shit just made me even more upset. Instead of cursing her out like I wanted to, I decided to take heed to her ending our conversation.

"If something happens to me because of your flawed process that's on you. Thank you for nothing. Have a good day."

I pressed the END button and sat my phone on the sofa cushion beside me. My mind roamed and I pictured Lauryn showing her ass in the parking lot of Phillip's Arena. How fucked up would that shit be? I was sure it would make Ari decide not to fuck with me anymore. Lauryn had already ran my ex Crystal away. Well, I couldn't just blame her. I wasn't the best boyfriend to her either. I was constantly accusing her of being with other men. Not only that, but I was cheating on her left and right. Why did I deserve a faithful woman when I was living like I was a single man? I had to do right by Ari, because I really wanted her in my life.

* * *

Stunting in front of the mirror, I had to admit that I was a nice looking man. True, I was vain, conceited even, but I'd earned it. I took care of myself and made sure that my appearance was always up to par. Shit, you only live once, so I was going to leave an impression while I was here. After I sprayed on my signature Gucci cologne, the sound of the doorbell startled me.

I wasn't expecting anybody. Ari was meeting me there, or did she change her mind. Was she spontaneous enough to surprise me? Maybe she'd tried to call, but I had left my phone on the sofa. What if I had missed her call? A smile spread across my face and instead of checking my phone first, I made my way to the door.

When I peeked through the peephole I noticed that something was covering it. My instinct told me not to open the door, but maybe that was part of Ari's surprise. I decided to peek out of the window to see if I saw her car, but all I saw was my own vehicle sitting there in my driveway. Damnit. The doorbell rang again, so I decided to say fuck it and answer it.

"Fuck! What the hell Lauryn?" I proceeded to push the door closed, but she stepped inside before I could.

"You know I took a warrant and restraining order out against you right?" I asked.

She rolled her eyes. "Really Ty? You didn't have to go there? I came to apologize to you. Can you please drop the charges? I didn't mean to do that. I'm so sorry. I let my emotions take over..."

"Wow, I can't believe you." I shook my head and cleared my throat. "Did you really think I'd buy the bullshit you're selling woman? I sell bullshit for a living, so I'm good at smelling it. Don't try it. I'm not dropping shit. You meant to hit me with that damn rock because it was already in your hand. I'm not going to turn my back on you right now, because I know how sneaky you can be, but you need to leave right now before I call the cops."

Tears filled her eyes and her bottom lips trembled pitifully. That shit kind of pulled at my heart strings for a second, but it didn't last. Suddenly I thought about the concussion that I'd suffered with. The headaches had been excruciating and I had a permanent scar to remind me of her psycho ass.

"No, I had the rock in my hand because I was moving it out of the driveway. I didn't want you to drive over it and mess up your tires. It just so happened that it was still in my hand and I reacted when you said what you said. You know I'd never hurt you Ty. I still love you and you know how it was when we were together. Well, how it was at first, before you changed." She cleared her throat. "I made a lot of mistakes, but I'd never hurt you on purpose Ty. You know that. I fucked up. Please, just accept my apology. I really want to try to work things out…"

"Please, just stop Lauryn. Look, okay, whatever. I accept your damn apology, but it's already in motion. I'm not dropping shit. I need you to just leave now. I have somewhere to go."

Her eyes scanned my body and then suddenly filled with something that I didn't recognize. Maybe it was just the eyes of a woman scorned.

"Where the fuck are you going?"

The door was still opened, so I pointed at it to make my point. "Where I'm going is my business and where you're going is yours. Get the hell out of my house now Lauryn or I'm gonna call the police. I'm not gonna warn you again. As a matter of fact, I'm just gonna walk away from you and trust that you do the right thing."

I shook my head and headed toward the bathroom in the hallway. After drinking a beer, I had to pee bad as hell. Hoping that she'd heeded my threat to call the cops, I left her there. After a few minutes I heard the door close. Letting out a sigh of relief, I washed my hands and left the restroom. She was gone and I was so damn glad.

I got myself together and decided to call Ari to let her know that I was on my way to meet her. When I walked over to the sofa to get my phone I noticed that it wasn't where I left it.

"Oh shit!" I ran toward to door to see if I could catch that crazy ass bitch.

There was no sign of her or a car in front of my house. Damnit!

"Lauryn! Lauryn!" I yelled like she would really come running back with my damn phone.

It felt like my head was going to explode. What the fuck could possibly happen next? Instead of dwelling on it, I decided to just go inside to grab my keys and continue on with my plans. I'd just have to get another phone in the morning Hopefully, I would somehow meet up with Ari in the crowd. I couldn't believe how crazy Lauryn was.

I went back inside, got my keys off the kitchen counter and locked up. My thoughts were all discombobulated as I made my way to my car. When I finally looked down I noticed that my front tire on the driver side was flat. When I crouched down to take a closer look I realized that it had been stabbed with something. That bitch!

"Arrrrrrrrrrrggggggggggggg!!!!" I yelled out in frustration.

I couldn't drive my car nor call Ari and explain thanks to Lauryn's crazy ass.

Chapter 6

Ari

By the time the third quarter was well underway the Hawks were beating the Knicks by 13 points and I knew that Tyson was not coming. I wasn't tripping though, however I was surprised that he hadn't even bothered to call and offer an explanation for standing me up. I started to question whether or not he was really feeling me, but decided to let time tell the story of his truth. If he was the man I thought he was he'd try to make amends for his little blunder. If he was the dog that most fine ass men such as him turned out to be, then he'd go on to pretend as if nothing happened, or he'd just completely blow me off. I didn't expect him to completely walk away from the opportunity to make me the center of his world, especially not before he could sample my goodies.

Arriving home later that evening I was still floored to have not heard anything from him. I started to call but then figured I'd make his ass sweat. He needed to know that I wasn't one of those docile little girls that got swept up in his charm and started chasing his ass. No, I was the prize. If anyone was going to be chased it would be me. I settled down for the evening and as my head hit the pillow I began to wonder how long it would be before I heard from Tyson's trifling ass.

As luck would have it, my wait wasn't long. Standing at my spot in teller window number three, I spotted the delivery person right away as he entered with a large assortment of balloons that said I'm sorry and a large Edible Arrangement basket. My little voice told me that it was for me. My manager, Camille, intercepted the delivery, exchanged words with the deliveryman, and then headed toward the teller area.

"Thank you ma'am. Is there anything else that I can assist you with today?" I asked the customer that was standing in front of me for whom I'd just completed a deposit.

"Can I get my balance?" The woman asked.

"Sure." In my mind I was wondering why she was so eager to know how little money she really had. I'd waited on the woman before and she'd never had more than $200.00 in her account at one time.

From my peripheral I could see Camille standing behind me with the basket and balloons in her hands. "Okay, your current balance is $167.53." I printed the receipt with that exact information on it and handed it to the woman.

She glared at it and then looked at me with a frosty expression as if I'd made a mistake. "Nuh-uh, why's it so low?"

Perhaps you should check your spending habits, I thought. I smiled politely. "You can always check your debit and credit history online or via the Bank of America app."

"Did you not credit my money to my account right?"

Now she was on my nerves. If she wanted to be pissed with someone about her lack of funds then she should be pissed with herself. Coming in there throwing a tantrum with me was not going to add any coins to her account. "Your full $50.00 deposit was credited to your account per the receipt that I just gave to you. If you'd like to learn how to better manage your funds then feel free to make an appointment and one of our personal bankers would be glad to sit down with you." This was me professionally advising her ass to get away from my window.

"Naw, you need to look at it again," she insisted.

I reached for the NEXT WINDOW sign and abruptly placed it on the counter in front of me. "Sorry. Your transaction has been completed. Feel free to make an appointment right over there for one of the bankers to assist you." I pointed over to the receptionist area where the sign in sheet was resting on a counter.

"Ari," my manager called my name from behind me.

I turned to face her without a care in the world. I was becoming sick of putting up with ratchet clients with no financial education whatsoever. Sure, my attitude was a little rude, but the customer's ignorance had warranted my lack of giving a fuck. "Yes?"

"Can I see you in my office?" She asked.

"Sure." I gave her an emotionless smile. I pointed to the gift in her hand. "I'm assuming you came over here because that's for me?"

"Oh, yes. Yes it is." She handed it to me as she looked over my shoulder at the customer who was still ranting and raving at the counter.

"This shit don't make no sense," the customer stated. "All I want is to know what's up with my money and you got this stuck up as skank up here acting like she better than somebody or something. Like she's too good to do her damn job."

"Ma'am, we'll have one of the personal bankers assist you immediately," Camille said approaching my teller window to diffuse the situation. "Please calm down and take a seat on the sofa over there." She picked up the phone extension at my window and quickly pressed a series of three numbers. "Curtis, please assist the older woman in the purple shirt now. Thank you."

I didn't care about the situation at all. Instead, I smiled at the Edible Arrangement in my hand as I poked a hole in the plastic to pull out the little card resting on the stick. I knew who it was from, but I was anxious to see what he had to say.

This fruit is only half as sweet as I'm hoping you'll be when it comes to accepting my apologies. Some crazy stuff happened, but none of it was a good enough excuse to miss out on the game with you. So, please be kind enough to meet me at this address tonight so that I can show you have sorry I truly am.

-Kicking myself a thousand times over,

Ty

I didn't recognize the address that he'd added on the card so I wondered where he was leading me to and how I should dress. I made a mental note to Google it later as I followed Camille into her office. I sat the arrangement down on her desk and took a seat in the chair across from it. She continued to stand behind her desk giving me a stern look that I found laughable. If she thought I was intimidated then she had another thing coming. I knew what I was working with and I knew who I was. There wasn't a chick alive –or dead for that matter – who could rock me in any way. I crossed my legs and smiled at her which I knew ate her up on the inside.

"What just happened with that customer was unacceptable," Nancy stated.

"Was it?" I asked astonished. I glanced down at my diamond studded watch and wondered if her rant was going to make me late for my lunch date.

"Yes it was. We don't argue with customers and—"

"I didn't argue with her by any means. I explained to her what happened and what she could do to further satisfy her inquiry. I wouldn't waste my breath arguing with anyone."

"We don't argue with customers *and* we certainly don't dismiss them without making sure that we've attended to all of their needs."

"I did attend to all of her needs to the best of my ability, and it's my lunch break. I'm a stickler for sticking to my schedule."

"Uh-huh, but for all extensive purposes, the way you handled that was not within Bank of America protocol. And speaking of protocol…something has been bothering me for the last month now."

"Is that right?"

"I've discussed it with the General Manager as well and the discretion to react was given to me. I've been tinkering with it for some time now, you know…trying to decide which way to go… but I think I've finally come to a conclusion."

She was getting on my nerves. Her inability to say what was on her mind made me want to choke her. She was unsure of herself, hence the rambling. I could remember a time when I was like that— timid, indecisive, unable to speak up for myself, and rather passive. Those days were long gone and had been kicked to the curb the moment I realized that quiet, docile women got fucked over readily and often.

"The day of the robbery you didn't follow protocol," Camille told me.

My left eyebrow rose. "Excuse me?"

"The alarm…it's right there by your teller window. You had every opportunity to reach down and press it while the robber was busy stealing money from Kelly's window. In fact, when we played the surveillance video back with the responding officers we noticed that the robber didn't come to your window at all."

I smiled politely. "So what is it that you're saying, Camille?" I asked. "Are you accusing me of having something to do with the robbery?"

"I'm saying that we found it odd that you didn't trip the alarm."

"The man had a gun. I was stunned just like every other person in the bank at the time, even you. I seem to remember you cowering on the floor near one of the banker's cubicles. Why didn't you pull your cell out and dial 911."

"Because that isn't standard procedure when you're being robbed."

"So, because I was afraid and didn't trip the alarm you're what? Going to write me up? Issuing me a warning?"

"No. We're going to have to let you go."

I was astonished, but in all honesty I didn't really care. I knew from the moment that I'd applied for the job that I wouldn't be there long. It was simply a means to an end. If they had the lack of vision to fire someone of my keen ability, know-how, and work ethic, then so be it.

"You're firing me? Because I didn't press the alarm?"

"That and we certainly will not tolerate the way that you address the customers. You're not...friendly."

I couldn't stifle my laugh. "You're firing me because I'm not friendly? That's bullshit and you know it."

"Your language is unacceptable."

"If you're going to do a big girl thing like terminate an employee the very least that you could do is be confident in your delivery. Tell the truth. I don't have to be friendly to stand out there and average shorter transaction times and more transactions completed than any of your other tellers. I'm good at what I do. I know it and you most certainly know it. You're letting me go because you and the officer investigating the robbery I suppose, have concluded that I'm somehow connected to what happened. And that, Nancy, is some bullshit. I'll tell you what, you can keep your little teller position. I'm aiming for bigger and better. And should we ever meet again I'm really hoping that I'm in no position of power because trust, I'd have just as much mercy upon and faith in you as you have with me right now." I rose from my seat and picked up the surprise that Tyson had sent.

"You don't get it do you?" Camille asked.

I looked at her as if she'd just grown a second nose.

"I'm not saying you had something to do with the robbery. We are a company that prides itself on morals, ethics, teamwork…we're a family here. You've never quite fit into that realm and your inability to follow protocol caused one of the team members…a member of the family if you will…it caused her her life. Kelly's dead, Ari. And had you followed protocol the police would have been here sooner and that unfortunate event wouldn't have happened. We simply can't keep you with such disregard for protocol."

I nodded. So now she was blaming me for Kelly's murder. So be it. I was fired and I'd just have to deal with it. "Thank you for the opportunity," I told her as I turned to exit the office. If I hurried I could still be on time for my lunch date.

***

"What took you so long?" He asked.

"Something came up at work and I needed to take care of it," I said as I slid into the booth at Ruby Tuesdays. "You already ordered?"

"Yeah, just an appetizer. So, what you got for me?"

I studied Darius' facial features as he stared at me with his dark and brooding eyes. He was a man that was about his business. Anyone else would have stammered over their words and felt ill at ease around him. He gave off the type of aura that gave people the impression that if you so much as sneezed around him, or blinked the wrong way he'd shoot you. I laughed at the thought because it was probably true. Darius wasn't someone you wanted to play with. I'd met him years before in Florida before I made the decision to return to Atlanta. He'd done some body guard work for someone close to me and over time I'd come to learn a lot about him and his hood upbringing as well as his thoroughness and loyalty. I trusted Darius explicitly and was damn lucky that the guy trusted me in return.

"Tell me again why your take isn't sufficient enough?" I questioned. Even though we had mutual trust and respect for one another, I was aimed to use my funds wisely. If I could hold on to some money I was going to hold on to it. Unnecessary spending wasn't my thing. Yes, I liked nice things and never rocked anything that you'd see the next chick wearing. Yes, I lived in a condo that many my age probably couldn't even afford. But, trust, everything I had had been gotten through serious blood, sweat, and tears that brought back memories I couldn't bear to face. I wasn't about spending no money or little money. I was about spending the right amount of money in the right places.

"It ain't sufficient 'cause me and prison don't mesh, Ma," he explained to me. "My earnings from the take, that shit's a bonus. Nonrefundable. The fee you owe me compensates for my time and the risk factor."

I understood him completely. Over time I'd learned that Darius had spent six years in prison for assaulting a man that had disrespected his sister and caused her to commit suicide. After his stint, he'd returned to the streets of Baton Rouge where he was from and finished what he'd started. The sister's ex was later found floating face down in a bayou. Soon after, Darius had migrated to Miami. Ever since then, he was hired by people with money to do the jobs that no one wanted to mention aloud and he was very good at what he did. I respected his ruthlessness and his time. As such, I pulled the envelope from my pocket and pushed it over to him. He'd done me a solid recently and had gone the extra mile just because I'd asked him to.

Darius took the envelope and stuck it inside of his jacket pocket. "Pleasure," he said quickly.

"Always. You sticking around for a while?"

Darius had been laying low for the last month, waiting for the day that we could make this exchange. He'd considered it his vacation as he parlayed in a hotel room where even I didn't know the location of.

"Catching a flight in two hours. Just needed to finish this business."

I nodded. "Understandable."

He looked at me and I almost wondered if that was compassion that I saw in his eyes. "Ari, you know what you doing?"

I cocked my head to the side. "I'm not second guessing myself. Would you second guess yourself?"

The appetizer arrived and the waiter asked if I was ready to order. I declined and he walked away.

"You know how to reach me if you need anything," Darius told me, dropping the concerned bit. "Try not to need me."

"I'm good," I assured him. "I'd love to stay, but I really need to get going. I have a mystery date to prepare for."

"Dude's pulling out all the stops, huh?"

I smiled. "And what? You thought he wouldn't? Look at me."

"I see you."

I laughed. "Right. You probably don't see anybody."

"Love is for the weak. I ain't got time for it."

Weak. The word made me cringe. It was a character trait that I vowed never again to have. I rose from my seat in the booth and smiled at my long-time friend. "Til next time," I told him.

"Later rather than sooner."

"Indeed."

***

"Ren?" I spoke loudly into the speaker phone as I took my time applying my makeup.

"Yeah?" She replied.

"So, what's the story? It's been quiet on my end today."

"I did what you asked me to do. It worked out didn't it?"

"That it did, but what exactly did you do?"

"Honestly, I was just myself."

"Well, you must have really done a knock-out job of being yourself because I haven't gotten a call all day."

"Um…yeah…about that. I have something for you. I thought it would maybe land me a bonus or something."

I put my lipstick brush down and studied my image in the mirror. Immaculate. I was stunning in my form fitting white tube dress with the light pastel makeup adorning my face. Less was always more. Some of the drag queen looking chicks I encountered on a daily basis didn't quite seem to get that. For a woman that had just been fired earlier in the day I sure as hell looked like a million bucks.

"Why, oh why are you trying to squeeze more money out of me?" I asked with a hint of annoyance. "Do I not do enough for you?"

"Hello? Have we met? I'm in a bind here, Ari. Plus, I think you're going to find this little souvenir beneficial."

"Have it on my doorstep within the next hour." I knew I was leaving and wouldn't have to be bothered with entertaining her when she showed up.

"Great. Text me the addy."

"Mmmhmmm. This better be worth all that you're saying it is."

"How much will you give me?"

I smirked. It always amazed me what others would do for a mere handout. "I'll decide that once I see what the hell it is."

Ren huffed. "Fine. I'll have it there in an hour."

"And Ren? Once you leave this don't make it a habit coming by my place okay?"

"Right," she stated.

I hung up and then quickly texted her my address. The truth was that I was anxious to see whatever it was that Ren thought would be so important to me. I took a final look at my figure and then sashayed out of the house to meet up with Tyson. It irked me a little that he still hadn't called all day although he'd sent the cute arrangement and the card with instructions to meet him. Still, it would have been nice of him to actually call and voice his apology rather than expect his little card to do the trick.

As I drove through the city to head to the downtown address he'd given me, my mind was a blur. I'd lost my job which meant that it was time for me to kick things into high gear. I needed to know where things were going with Tyson and in order to figure out how long I could actually keep my current life going. Miami was calling to me and I knew that I was going to have to return home soon. But the duration of my stay in Atlanta greatly depended upon Tyson. Progress had to be made.

I parked my car in a lot off of Peachtree Street and then walked down the block to the corner address where I was to meet Tyson. I held my clutch purse close to me feeling some kind of way about his man asking me to meet him out on a corner in the middle of the evening. It was just past eight and the sun had gone down. The downtown nightlife was beginning to stir and people were everywhere—walking and in cars, heading to this club or that lounge in order to enjoy the best of whatever entertainment and spirits that Atlanta had to offer. I started to call Tyson's phone to ascertain that his ass was where he said he'd be, but the sight of a huge white lace and carriage lit up with clear lights caught my eye. It was attached to a beautiful white pony and standing beside it, petting the animal lovingly, was a man dressed in a slacks and a crisp button up looking as if he'd just stepped off of the pages of GQ Magazine.

I was speechless as I approached the scene and saw Tyson's beautiful smile welcoming me. Looking to my left I saw what had to be over two dozen white roses resting on the seat of the carriage. "What is all this?" I asked breathlessly.

"This," Tyson said approaching me and pulling me to an embrace that had me wanting to grab his dick and claim it as mine. "…is me saying how very…" He kissed my forehead. "…very…" He kissed the tip of my nose. "…very…" He kissed both of my cheeks. "…very sorry that I am for last night." His lips covered mine and my body melted from the passion of the moment.

For a second I forgot that we were out on the street as I threw my arms around his neck and pressed my body closely against his muscular frame. This man was damn near irresistible. His kiss had me burning from the inside out with cardinal desire that I knew would make the ordinary woman go stupid. His hands cupped my ass and I was so glad that I had elected not to wear any panties.

"Damn," he said as he pulled his lips away from mine. "Baby, you are so fuckin' delicious. I wanna taste the rest of you."

I smiled coyly. "I bet you do."

Tyson motioned to the carriage where the driver sat ready and waiting. "Your chariot awaits, my love. I want to carry you all over the city tonight at a leisurely pace to make up for every moment I missed of the game last night. Tonight belongs to you."

I smiled. He was trying to get the drawers. He'd gone above and beyond and that cocky look on his face was telling me that he just knew he was getting his dick wet tonight. *Hmmm*, I thought. *Maybe*.

Chapter 7

Tyson

During our carriage ride around the city we enjoyed the bright lights and the feel of Atlanta. It was certainly a place to party and enjoy the finer things in life. All I wanted to do was take her to the W and return the favor that she'd bestowed upon me the other night, among other things. However, she was a woman who deserved to be romanced to the point of no return. When I did get it, I wanted to savor it.

"So, what happened last night?" She asked as we approached the restaurant where I'd made reservations.

We would have our own little private area to dine and I was hoping that she'd be impressed enough to let me finally sample her goodies.

I sighed. "I lost my damn phone…"

"How did that happen?" She asked staring back at me with doe like eyes.

I had to catch my breath. She was so damn beautiful that it was unrealistic.

"I don't know. I think I left it on the counter when I ran to CVS last night. It wasn't like I could call down there and when I got to my car I noticed that I had a damn flat. No garages were open that late, so I sucked up my lack of communication and transportation hoping I'd get to make it up to you right away." I kissed her hand after I let the lie slip pass my lips. She didn't need to know about what had happened with Lauryn last night.

I'd reported her rude intrusion and theft to the police. They claimed to be on it and I hoped that they got her ass before her antics started to interfere with my relationship with Ari. After getting my car towed to the garage, I caught a taxi to Verizon to turn the phone off that Lauryn had stolen and got a new one.

Once I picked my car up I made reservations at Bones and the W. I'd already gone to the room to make it romance ready. There were rose petals leading from the door to the bedroom. There was also a bottle of Ace of Spades chilling in the mini bar/fridge.

"Oh wow, that's crazy. It's like the universe was against us being together last night." She smiled up at me and it radiated her already gorgeous facial features.

"Yeah, but the universe ain't got shit on destiny. Nothing's gonna keep me from being with you Ari. I have deemed you as mine now, so fuck the universe. It's all about us baby." With that said I kissed her awaiting lips lightly.

When her tongue slipped between mine it was like my body was instantly on fire. She was igniting something in me that I'd never felt. When we finally separated I decided to ask her about her day and she told me about what had happened at her job.

"Jealous bitch," she added at the end. "I knew that Camille had it out for me. She looks at me and sees what she wishes she could've been at my age with her old ass. I hate older women. They're always intimidated by me and the younger ones aren't any better."

"You gonna be good though? I mean, do you have some money saved up. If not…I got you. I mean…I ain't broke or nothing. I'm good with my funds."

"I know," she said with a flirtatious smile. "But fortunately I'm just as responsible as you are, so I'm good for now. I'll find something else soon, so no worries over here. Let's just enjoy tonight, okay."

I nodded having not one problem with her request. "Cool."

Just as I said that, the carriage stopped.

"Well my lady." I beamed at her. "This is the end of our ride. Now it's time for some grub."

"Oh, okay. Wow Ty." Her eyes lit up when she realized where we were. "You're really going all out huh?"

"You already know that nothing's too good for you. I can tell by how you carry yourself."

When I stepped out of the carriage I walked over to her side, grabbed her hand and helped her step out.

"Well," she looped her arm into mine. "You're very observant to be a man. Usually y'all let most things fly over your heads."

"Oh no sexy. If anything my head has been filled with thoughts of you. Literally. And speaking of head, yours is the best. Hands down. Got me trying to wife your ass and I ain't even had the goods yet."

She blushed as I led her toward the door of one of Atlanta's most expensive eateries. Bones was a steakhouse located on Piedmont Rd. It was hella expensive, but after standing my boo up, I had to pull out all of the stops. Besides, I had a little splurge money in my account anyway. It wasn't like I couldn't spend a little something without hurting.

"Well, I really appreciate you making last night up to me. Those tickets weren't cheap sir." She kissed my cheek as I chuckled.

"I know sweetheart, so order whatever you want. I mean that."

She tightened her grip on my arm. "Hmm, I can eat, so be careful what you ask for."

I gave her a flirtatious smile and a wink as I snuck a peek at her fat ass. It was obvious that she'd been eating good. "I can eat too ma and if everything goes as planned you'll experience my skills firsthand."

"Well damn." She flashed a look at me that made my blood boil, and not in a bad way.

"Oh, believe me, that's gonna be your favorite word tonight."

We both laughed as we made our way inside of the fancy restaurant like the happy, power couple that I planned for us to be.

* * *

"Fuck! Damn…oh…my…God…Ty…!" Her eyes were rolling back in her head and I knew that getting that room at the W was going to seal the deal. When she saw the rose petals her face was pleasantly surprised. After a few glasses of Ace of Spades her legs were spread eagle and I was feasting on her succulence.

Okay, so I still hadn't sampled that pussy yet, but my face was all up in it. Mmm, Mami's kitty cat was just right. That thang was waxed clean, plump and so pretty. When I undressed her and had the chance to see all of that beauty unmasked, it was over for a nigga. I was officially gone over the edge of the cliff. Mami's body was beyond perfection. That shit was enough to make a grown man cry like a bitch.

Her C cup breasts were round and her nipples were large and so inviting. I instantly had one in my mouth before I could get her dress off good. Her waist was slender, but her hips blossomed out like a flower in full bloom. Her thighs were amazingly thick and soft and her feet were small and delicate. Damn, even her feet were pretty. Then the pussy on her. Oh my goodness. Was I really that lucky? Pretty face, blemish free body. Ari was a fucking goddess in the flesh and I was feasting on that sweet pussy like I hadn't just finished off an expensive ass dinner.

"Mmm, ma, you taste so damn sweet. Such a decadent dessert," I whispered as I cupped her full ass cheeks in my hands.

In no time her hands were grabbing at my head and she was moaning loud as hell.

"Mmm, ohhh...uhhh...damn! I'm cumming! Damn Ty!" She screamed and her juices flowed from her like a fountain.

When I was done slurping it all up I finally came up to kiss her sexy ass lips. Well, the ones on her face. Her eyes were glazed over and she looked mesmerized.

"Damn," she said in a low, breathless voice.

"Told you that was going to be your favorite word tonight," I said and kissed her soft lips again.

She was out of breath as she spoke. "I see that you were confident in your skills, but when most men brag, they don't deliver."

"I keep showing you that I'm not like most men then huh?"

She stared into my eyes with a serious look on her face that I couldn't read. "Yeah, I guess so."

It was silent in the room for a minute before either of us spoke.

"Well, I ain't gonna lie." I let my hand find its way to her warm, wet center.

I pushed my pointer finger inside of her tightness gently as I leaned over to kiss her. After sucking her bottom lip, I pulled away and continued.

"I want to feel you so bad. Ari, I need to be inside of you right now like I need to fucking breathe. My life depends on it." I let out a sigh as I whispered seductively in her ear.

I could feel her body shiver and her sexy voice was low and throaty. "I want you inside of me too Ty. What's stopping you?" She laid back and reached out to wrap her small hand around my tightness.

"Mmm." I added my middle finger to my teasing and she licked her lips.

"Ohhh…your fingers feel so good…"

I stared down at her. "Just wait 'til you feel this dick."

"Still talking shit I see." Her eyes were on mine, challenging me.

"Oh, I'm 'bout to back it up ma."

I reached over and removed a box of condoms from the nightstand.

"So, you just knew you were getting some huh?" She'd asked in a playful way, but I knew that she was serious.

I chuckled. "Nah, I got them just in case. There was no way that I wasn't going to be ready."

She grabbed my face and tongued me down. "Alright. Well, give me the dick already. I'm wet as hell."

I slid the condom down the shaft of my hard dick, turned on by how aggressive and outspoken she was being. I could tell that she wasn't going to be a boring lay. Judging from how she was gyrating and bucking that ass when I was eating that pussy, she was not going to be lazy. I was prepared for her to throw that fat ass back to me and I was ready to catch it.

I positioned myself on top of her and her soft hands slowly grazed my back. "You sure you can handle this? My pussy's better than good. If you think you're into me now, it's about to be over for you sexy," she said with her eyes still on mine.

Damn, I had to look away. Ma did have me fucked up already. I was almost scared. Shit, I was literally about to throw away my player's card to try and be a one woman man. When I looked down at my prize it was worth it. I had to bag her before another man did.

"Oh, that's the plan ma. I'm ready to be whipped and I wanna fall in love. Just prepare for the feeling to be mutual because I don't play with the pussy, I please it." My lips were on her neck as I slowly entered her.

"Oh really?" She asked.

"Hell yeah." I breathed into her neck.

The initial shock of her wet, heat made me take in a sharp breath. She was so fucking tight, but eating her pussy had made it so that entry wasn't so hard.

"Fuck…" She took in a sharp breath.

I stopped. "Am I hurting you?"

"Kinda," she whispered. "It's been a while for me."

"I'm sorry. I'll take my time ma. Relax for me. I'm not tryna hurt it. Open your legs a little bit more."

She repositioned her legs and then I started to lick and suck all over her neck and breasts. In no time I was inside, nice and snug. Oh, she felt so fucking good. At first she wasn't really moving. I guess she had to get used to my length and girth. After a while she was moaning and throwing it back to me with each thrust. Lil' mama was into it.

"Ohhh…Ari…damn, you were right ma. This pussy's hella good. Mmm…"

Her hands were on my ass, squeezing as I grinded up in that pussy in deep circles.

"Uhhh…shit…Ty…damn…" I stared down at her enjoying her faces of bliss. "That's my spot. Uhh…damn…you're gonna make me cum…"

She was biting her bottom lips as her eyes rolled back in her head.

"Yeah, cum all over daddy's dick wit' your sexy ass." I was feeling myself, but I was also feeling that pussy biting back. It was gripping my dick like no other and if I didn't hold it together I was going to be cumming too.

"Ohhh…ohhh…I'm…I'm…cumming Ty!!!!"

I flipped her over so that she was on her stomach.

"Put that ass up in the air!" I slapped each of her fat ass cheeks and then dived right back in.

Fuck that. I had to put it down the first time. That cumming fast shit wasn't in the plan. Nah. My mission was to have her gone over the "D" like she said I'd be over her ass. All I could do was stare down at that fat ass as it jiggled. Ohh, I was balls deep in that pussy and my dick was tingling like crazy. She kept on moaning and screaming, sounding all sexy. I couldn't hold it in any longer. It was over for me.

"Ohhh....Ohhhh....uhhhh....mmm...I 'm cumming again!"

That was my cue. I grabbed her around the waist and pulled her into me. She couldn't even move because I was all up in those guts.

"Fuck Ty! Shit!"

"Ma...fuck! I'm 'bout to cum!" I went in even harder and then I felt it. Oh yeah, it was the best nut of my existence. "Ari...Argggghhhh! DAMN!"

My body got so weak that I couldn't help but collapse on top of her.

"Mmm, that was good as hell, but I can't breathe Ty..."

I lifted up, slapped her on that fat ass again and headed toward the bathroom.

"Yup, I'm whipped ma," I confessed on the way. "I'm ready for round two."

She laughed. "That shit was awesome, but I'm beat babe. Maybe in the morning."

I was disappointed, but that was cool. "A'ight, but get used to stamina if you're gonna be with me." I flushed the condom and then washed my hands.

When I reentered the room she was laying there with her legs wide open like she was letting that monkey cool off.

"So, it's official? You're my man now? Exclusively?" She asked before standing up.

My hands moved up and down her thighs as I took in her sexy, curvaceous frame. Damn, I was the luckiest man on the planet. That shit was all mine. Mmm, I planned to do all types of nastiness to her.

"Hell yeah. I'm your man and you're my woman exclusively. I ain't trying to fuck with nobody else and I expect for you not to be either. I'm falling for you and now that we've consummated the relationship, it's official. You think I'm letting your fine ass go. Hell fuck nah. Your ass is mine now," I explained more clearly for her that time.

She put her hands on my shoulders and leaned over to give me a sweet kiss. I sucked her tongue and squeezed her soft ass before she pulled away.

"So, that means that you're ready for your life as a bachelor to be over? Are you sure? I mean, if you want we can just be friends with benefits. I don't want to…"

I looked up at her with sincerity in my eyes. "I want to be with you Ari. How many times do I have to tell you that? I already know what comes with us being in an exclusive relationship and I'm ready for it.

What happened at the bank and Lauryn attacking me just showed me that I need to try something different. I need to settle down because life is too damn shòrt. I want to enjoy my time here with somebody special. Not every chick that I see. That ain't me no more. I'm a changed man. Thanks to you."

"Aww babe. Okay, so there. We're official." She gave me a quick peck on the lips before running off to the restroom.

A big giddy grin spread across my face as I heard the sound of her singing and then the water running. In no time I was snoring.

Chapter 8

Ari

I was singing alright. Singing with the joy of knowing that I had Tyson Reid right where I wanted him. I hadn't expected to give up the cookies that night, but something told me that I needed an extra edge to make sure that I had him hooked. The way his eyes roamed my body and snuck peeks at my ample ass at every given opportunity, I knew that he was lusting for the pussy—practically dying for it. I'd be lying if I said that I wasn't interested in finding out exactly what the all grown up, player had to offer.

Besides, I'd been so engrossed in work and living out my plans that I hadn't been properly fucked in way too long. My body needed to release some tension and my purple Pearl Rabbit vibrator just wasn't going to do the trick anymore. Feeling Tyson all up in it did wonders for me. It gave my body the physical attention that it craved and me the satisfaction of knowing that he was all mine. Yep, Tyson was now a one woman man and I was that lucky woman.

By the time I arrived home I knew that I had some wheels to set in motion. Time was of the essence especially since I was no longer employed at Bank of America. Approaching my front door, I noticed a small package leaning up against the black steel door. A smile spread across my face and I couldn't help but to laugh to myself. I knew what was in that package. I scooped it up and hurried inside to take yet another shower and change into some comfortable clothing. I made myself a cup of green tea before settling down at my desk in front of my computer for the day. I had some things to do starting with checking my funds.

When I'd told Tyson that I too was financially responsible it hadn't been a lie. In fact, it was probably an understatement. At 28 years old I was probably one of the wealthiest females of my generation that I knew. I had to learn early on about capitalizing on opportunities, survival of the fittest, diversifying my funds once I received them, and taking control of all aspects of my life including my financial wellbeing. These lessons were all taught to me in a very cruel and harsh way that I generally tried to block out of memory. But, no matter how hard I tried to forget my past I simply couldn't. In fact, it was a large part of the reason as to why I was back in Atlanta anyway. It was time to face some of my demons; time to put some things to rest so that I could move on.

I checked my general checking and savings, the accounts of which I accessed for my general day to day living. Nothing rested below six figures. I then checked my mutual funds to make sure that they were still accruing nicely. Satisfied with what I saw, I went on to check my Capital One Orange savings account, the account that I used as an untouchable savings. The number had grown since depositing my most recent check and I smiled. For the rest of my life that account would only grow fatter and I planned to run off to some tropical island and live carefree off of my earnings before long. Taking a sip of my tea, I logged into my credit union account to see where my special checking account rested. I'd opened it specifically to fund the current project that I was working on. I'd withdrawn nearly $30,000.00 from my untouchable savings accounts just to open up the project checking account. I figured an average person's annual salary was enough to complete the tasks associated with this project. That $30,000.00 was dwindling. The account now rested at $16,000.00. I'd vowed not to spend a penny more of my money on this plan so it was time to make this last half of the funds truly work for me and get on with it.

I entered my email account and schemed through correspondences until I found who I was looking for. Yasmin Flowers. She was on my mind. We'd met online via a Facebook group that served as a virtual support group of people with life-threatening illnesses. At the time, I'd only been trying to support Reginald, someone very close to me who was a member of the group and was practically on his death bed. I would sit online for hours reading the interactions between the people in this group and feeling some kind of way about the stories they would share.

Yasmin's testimony touched me the most as she shared how she'd been violently abused by a man she'd loved with all of her soul. It tore at my heart strings and angered me to read about how he'd rape her and belittle her over and over again until finally she got the strength and the courage to break free of the imprisonment of their poisonous relationship. Yet, the tragic twist of learning that he'd given her AIDS had pretty much left Yasmin scarred with the memory of this man's cruelty forever. The way people treated others sometimes really made my blood boil.

The way men treated women specifically made me vengeful. Why didn't men understand how precious a woman's love could be? Why didn't men understand how special it was when a woman offered herself to a man, emotionally and physically?

For nearly a year I'd kept in contact with Yasmin, helping to fund her medical care and trying my best to keep her spirits lifted. I didn't have AIDS, but I certainly understood how crushed she felt having been so mistreated and so fatally scorned by the one man she loved more than life itself.

During this year, Yasmin had opened up to me in ways that she'd never opened up to anyone else, telling me thoughts, feelings, and ideas that others would have seen as criminal, demonic, and cruel. I didn't pass any judgment at all. I totally understood. In turn, I'd shared more with Yasmin about my life than I had with anyone else other than Reginald. Our relationship was special and I wouldn't have expected anyone else to understand it. So thankful for my kindness, generosity, and sincerity Yasmin often vowed that she'd do any and everything for me. I always knew the day would come where I'd actually need her to follow through. In fact, I'd spent several months setting it up so that when the time came all systems would be a go.

I smiled as I sent a short reply to
Yasmin's last email:

Hey boo thang,

Hope all is well with you and that you're
good to go. Sorry haven't been able to get
up with you here lately, but it's been very
busy on my end. Be prepared for it to go
down soon. In the meantime, make that
money!

- Ari

I hit the send button and then reached
for the package that had been left for me
the night before. Tearing it open, I
smirked as I realized the possibilities that
this little gift held in store for me. Pulling
out the small device and holding it in my
hand, I pressed the side button out of
curiosity. Lucky for me, it was still

charged although only at thirty-six percent. I wasted no time in scrolling through the messages yet finding nothing of interest, I decided to hurry over to the gallery before the power died. I laughed out loud at the common ratchetry before my eyes: pictures of women's asses, tits, and pussy shots. No doubt some very loose women with little to no self-respect had been sure that this was a way of getting the attention that they craved. An idea occurred to me the moment I saw a dick that I recognized as if I'd just seen it yesterday. *Hmmm*, I thought. *A bragging individual makes for an arrogant individual who no doubt would love to have their prize on display.* The thought tickled me.

I reached for my cell to make a call, but was dismayed to have the phone begin ringing in my hand. I wasn't pissed because I was receiving a call. I was annoyed because it was my mother who was no doubt calling to bother me once again about coming to visit. Didn't she understand that we didn't have that type of relationship? Didn't she realize that I wasn't ready to let bygones be bygones?

"Yes mother?" I answered the phone not caring to mask my attitude.

"Oh, I'm sorry," she said meekly. "I…I just assumed that you'd be at work. I was planning to leave a message."

"Well I'm not," I said snappily. "What is it?"

"You um…you got something in the mail. Um, an invitation from Carver High."

I knew what it was. The memory of it only agitated me more. I didn't know why I hadn't expected it to arrive since I knew all about it. It only goes to show how much I'd removed myself from that era of my life. "Thanks. You can toss it," I told her.

"You sure? Maybe it's time that you—"

"Let me go ahead and clear something up so that we don't have to keep rehashing this, okay?" I interjected. "I appreciate what you're trying to do here, but I don't want it. I can't foster a relationship with you right now under these false pretenses."

"False pretenses?"

"You want to act like nothing happened? You want to act like your super religious beliefs aren't anything more than cult mentality? You want to pretend like you didn't toss your only child, your daughter, to the wolves simply to save yourself from the embarrassment of your church family? Your bullshit ass community!"

"I only did what I thought was best for you! I saved your life child."

"You saved my life?" Memories of excruciating pain flooded back to me. Mental snapshots of blood dripping from my body, a faceless man ripping away at my womanhood, and cold lonely nights crying out in the dark for a mother who simply wasn't there physically or emotionally. "My life is good now and that is all because of me. Please, don't fool yourself into believing that you've done me any favors. If you've done anything for me, you've taught me that I don't need anyone but me. Do me a solid okay? Don't call me back." I hesitated for a moment, feeling the sharpness of my verbal sparring. I softened just a little. "When I'm ready, if ever I'm ready, I'll come to you."

Before she could respond I pressed the END button and went on with my call to Ren. My facial expression was emotionless as I listened to the phone ringing in my ear and stared at my computer screen. I refused to allow past emotions to resurface and cloud my judgment. I was on a mission. I was in the middle of working my plan. I was in the middle of overcoming. I was not that docile little girl anymore who desperately needed someone to love and care for me nor was I the naïve teenager who had no clue what to do with her life. I was in control now. I was Ari Smit, a redefined, much stronger version of myself than anyone from my past could ever be used to.

"Finally," Ren greeted me. "You got the package?"

My mood lifted just a little. "I did, I did. You are quite resourceful and a quick thinker. I like that."

"Hmmm. Is it useful to you?"

"It is actually. Thank you."

"Part of the favor right? So what's next? I really need to get that money."

"Tell you what, I'm going to go ahead and deposit the funds into your account today."

"What?" Ren was astonished. "So what? I'm done?"

"Just about. I need you to make a phone call and get a list for me."

"That's it?"

"That's it. I'll text you the name of the establishment and the specific list that I want you to get for me. Make sure I get that within the next couple of days okay? In the meantime, you'll have your money today." I trusted Ren to do this last favor. Besides, it was a breeze.

"Thank you! I'll get right on it."

"Mmmhmm. Take care of yourself, Ren. Make good choices," I advised her, having no plans to ever contact her again after receiving this last favor. "I'm sending the text now."

"Thank you," she said again. "Thank you so much!"

I ended the call and quickly sent her the last assignment I'd need her to complete.

Carver High School....class of 2005
mailing list

I rose from the desk, dropped my newly acquired device over in my purse, and used my cell to dial Tyson's number as I headed for the door. I needed to make a quick trip to Wal-Mart's photo center.

"Hey beautiful," Tyson answered for me.

I smiled. "Hey handsome."

"I was just about to go into the office and fill out some paperwork with a customer."

"Oh you made a sale. Good for you!"

"You know how I do."

His cockiness made me roll my eyes as I slid into the driver's seat of my car.

"What are you up to?" He asked me.

"On my way to a job interview," I lied. "Just thought I'd check in and see how my man was doing."

"Awww. Thanks, bae. I'm gonna have to hit you back when I'm done here."

"No, no…it's okay. I'm not sure how long I'll be out. But, I do want to take you somewhere tonight, if you're up for something a little…kinky."

"Shitttt," he whispered into his phone, probably so that his customer couldn't hear his vulgarity or his excitement. "I'm always down for some kinky shit, especially with your fine ass."

I backed out of my spot and headed toward my destination, still holding the phone to my ear. "Okay, boo. I'll pick you up at your place around eight tonight, okay?"

"What? And you chauffeuring a brother too? I know I've died and gone to heaven because no woman ever wants to drive a man around."

"Oh baby, you ain't seen nothing yet. You're with me now," I said seductively. "And your woman is full of surprises."

"Mmm. That's what's up. I'll see you tonight, sexy."

"Yep."

We ended the call and I zipped through the streets of Stone Mountain. Yeah, Tyson was in for a long lasting surprise that I knew he wasn't ready to handle.

***

As promised, I scooped Tyson up at eight o'clock and he reveled in the opportunity to ride in the passenger seat of my MKZ. He pressed me for information of our destination during the entire ride but I remained quiet about it. The high-waisted, slimming black shorts that I wore left my thighs completely exposed. Tyson took full advantage of this as he groped and caressed my legs, trying to slide his fingers into my crotch area to discretely stroke my kitty. I knew that he was fiending for the pussy and after he saw where I was taking him, I knew that he would be pre-ejaculating soon enough.

As we pulled into the parking lot, Tyson's eyes grew wide. "Mardi Gras?" He asked.

I smiled, but said nothing as I pulled the key from the ignition and got out of the car. He followed suit and grabbed my hand as I rounded the car.

"Bae, really?" He asked in amazement. "You brought me to a strip club?"

"Not a strip club," I corrected him. "One of the best strip clubs in Atlanta. Come on."

He was speechless as I led him under the awning to the front doors of the heavily populated club. We got through security and the hostess led us to the V.I.P. area upon hearing that I'd already requested a reservation. Soon, we were seated at a round table where a bottle of chilled Moet awaited us and a close up view of the stage provided us with the perfect vantage point to see the current dancer busting it wide open while sliding down the shimmering pole.

I poured us each a glass of champagne as I watched Tyson look around in awe. Beautiful half and fully naked women of all races sashayed around offering lap dances and most likely the promise of something a little extra if the money was right. Tyson sat back in his seat and stared at the dancer on stage with low eyes. I knew that his dick was getting hard. I'd become very familiar with his lustful expressions.

I handed him his glass. "You okay?" I loudly whispered into his ear over the music.

He took the glass, nodded, and looked me in my eyes. "Shit, I'm more than okay. I swear, I've never met a woman like you. You gotta be hella confident to bring your man to a strip club."

I smiled and kissed him passionately. "This is nothing but motivation," I told him. "For both of us," I added with a wink.

The twinkle in his eye let me know that he was thinking exactly what I wanted him to think, no matter how untrue it was. There was something about the possibility of a threesome, or watching your woman get sexed by another woman that made a man go wild. Tyson was no exception. He took a sip of his drink and returned his focus to the dancer as she ended her set.

"Damn baby, you really are full of surprises," he told me.

He really had no idea.

"Yep and I got another one for you too," I told him.

I made eye contact with a dancer standing near the bar and slightly nodded my head. I watched as she finished her drink and then glided over to our table. She was tall for a chick and her heels only made her taller. It was perfect to me. I knew that men liked tall women. She was dressed in a sequined black bra and a black wrap tied around her waist revealing a pair of long, fit legs. Her Brazilian weave flowed down her back and her face was beat to the gods. I didn't get down with women, but I had no problem giving credit where credit was due. This stripper was a bad bitch.

I looked over at Tyson and reached over to squeeze his thigh just as Beyoncé's 'Dance for You' began to blast through the speakers of the club. "Want a lap dance?" I asked him.

He shook his head nervously. Maybe he thought I was going to feel some type of way about another woman grinding against the hard-on that my fingers had already brushed up against.

"Naw, you ain't gotta do that," he told me, looking into my eyes as if he wanted to rip my clothes off right then and there.

I smiled and removed my hand from his lap. "Too late."

The stripper placed her hand on his head, leaned down, and lightly licked his right ear before seductively saying, "I'm Climaxx."

Before he could turn around to get a look at the woman who'd so boldly addressed him, Climaxx aggressively pulled back Tyson's chair with the strength of an Amazon. His eyes were wide and his mouth stood open as she wound her body to the beat of the music while standing between his legs. She licked her lips and threw her head back in a sexy manner as she loosened the knot on her wrap and quickly revealed the G-string that matched her bra. I saw Tyson swallow hard as he took in her large breasts and the swell of her hips showing her very plump ass. As Beyoncé crooned about rocking on her baby, Climaxx turned around and lowered her ass into Tyson's lap. She popped it as he looked down at it while biting his bottom lip.

Climaxx leaned back against his chest, put her arms up, and caressed his head as her ass continued to gyrate on beat against the rock in his pants. Seconds later she rose and turned to face him, straddled his left knee, and reached up to snap the front of her bra to expose her large nipples and dark areolas. Her shoulders swayed and her boobs jumped in tune just before she reached up and pulled Tyson's face down to inhale the baby powder fresh scent of her cleavage.

I knew that he was moments away from busting a nut in his pants and had to work hard to stifle my laugh. Climaxx never cracked a smile. She was serious about her work. I admired the way she worked her body and totally dominated the attention of most of the men in the V.I.P. section although her focus was on Tyson. The song persisted and so did Climaxx as she stood upright, placed at high heeled foot on the edge of Tyson's chair between his legs while spreading her own legs enough to give him a good view of her pussy. Her hips continued to gyrate as she pulled the thing fabric of her G-string to the side in order to thrust her exposed, shave pussy toward him.

Tyson's hands lingered in mid-air around Climaxx's body. I could tell that he was conflicted between grabbing her ass and trying to remain respectful to me. Climaxx was relentless. She rubbed her bare pussy against the fabric that barricaded his dick from making contact with her flesh. All she had to do was pull down his pants and they would have been as good as fucking with the way she moved on his body. She pushed Tyson's head back as she pressed her bare breasts against his chest while completely sitting in his lap with her legs around him and the chair. She humped him rhythmically until the song came to a sexy, dwindling end. She lingered in his lap for only a minute before hopping up and turning to me.

I handed her a twenty dollar bill and smiled. She took the cash, turned around to blow Tyson a kiss, and then walked away. I looked at Tyson and noticed the rise and fall of his chest as his eyes were glued to Climaxx's retreating, jiggling ass. Typical. Put some ass and pussy in front of a man and he would lose his mind. I was banking on that.

Chapter 9

Tyson

If I had known that being in a relationship could be so fulfilling, I'd committed to a chick a long time ago. Ari was the shit, but I was sure that I'd come across some good women in my past that I'd done wrong as hell. At least I had come to my senses just in time. The right woman had been sent to me and I was enjoying it.

It was my twenty eighth birthday and the festivities started at my parents' house. The tradition for our birthdays was for us to exchange gifts and have dinner early in the day. I'd invited Ari, but she said that she had to go out of town for a family emergency, but she'd be back in time for my class reunion. I was disappointed, but she said that she'd make it up to me by sending me something special later on.

"Happy birthday son," my father said with a proud smile on his face as he passed me a gift wrapped, rectangular box.

"Thanks old man," I grinned as I grabbed it and tore the wrapping paper off like a kid.

I popped the black, velvet box open and it was a platinum, diamond encrusted Rolex.

"Wow, what did I do to deserve this?" I asked my pops with wide eyes.

He chuckled good-naturedly as he patted me on the back. "I'm really proud of you son. Good job, your own house, no baby mamas hanging all over you. You know, it's hard to be a successful black man, but you make it look easy. I got some brisket on the grill, some cold beer and the game is about to come on..."

My mother cleared her throat and made her way over to us. "I have something for Tyson too. You always try to steal my thunder Jason."

Her hands were on her hips and her mahogany colored skin glowed with humor. "Here you are honey."

She passed me a much larger box that I took from her gratefully. I shook it and she laughed.

"I'm glad it's not fragile," she said before taking my father's hand.

I smiled at their show of affection and tore the wrapping paper off before neatly placing it beside me on the sofa. Honestly, I was just a little OCD, so I didn't want to make a mess.

When I opened the box a grin decorated my face. "Thanks ma. I've been wanting one of these."

It was a NutriBullet Blender and I was a sucker for fitness. All types of ideas for fruit and vegetable smoothies filled my mind. I was overdue to hit the gym, so it would somehow motivate me.

"Well, I need you to be healthy and fit so you can catch that wife and give us some grandbabies."

I grinned because she was right on time. "Well, I met somebody and I really…like her. To be honest, I'm falling in love with her."

My mother squeezed my father's hand as she glanced up at him lovingly. I'd always longed for what they had.

"When will we meet her then?" My mother asked. "This is a first for you. Hmm. Your brother and sister have already settled down, but you…I was worried."

My father chuckled. "He's a young man sweetheart. Give him time. He just said that he met somebody and I can't wait to meet her."

"Me either. What's her name?" Mother quizzed me as she wiped her hands on her white, lacey apron.

Pops was smoking the brisket, but she was handling the sides and dessert, which I hoped was her famous German Chocolate Cake.

"Ari and she is beautiful and smart." I couldn't help but picture her face. Damn, I missed her. "She is so laid back and drama free. I know that you two will love her."

"Where's she from?" Pops asked.

"Florida. She moved here a few months ago. I met her at the bank. She works there." Well, she did. I couldn't help but smile

My mother grinned back at me knowingly. "You look so happy baby."

Pops stood up. "Yes, he does. Do the two of you have plans tonight?"

"Nah, unfortunately she's out of town, but I'm sure she'll make it up to me. We just get along like that. She got it together and I'd like to think that I held out for her."

"There you go son," my father said before leaving the room.

When he returned he had two cold Bud Lights in his hand. "Let's watch the game. I'm ready to see the Hawks whoop some ass."

"Oh Lord," my mother said as she got up from the sofa. "Let me let you men do what you do while I go check on the food."

My pops and I went along with our manly banter as she left the room with her cell phone in hand. I figured she'd be chatting with my sister or gossiping with one of her church sisters to past the time. I couldn't wait to eat some of my parents' hearty, stick to your bones cuisine, but I was mostly looking forward to Ari's surprise.

* * *

When I got home it was a little after seven, but there wasn't a package or anything waiting for me from Ari. I was just a little bit disappointed, but I figured it would maybe be a day or so late. Either way it was the thought that counts. I decided to get comfy and stripped down to my boxers and white tee. Just as I was about to take my tee off, my doorbell rang.

'Who the hell could that be?' I asked myself as if I would get an answer without checking.

I looked out of the peephole hoping that it wasn't Lauryn. To my pleasant surprise it wasn't, but I wasn't expecting to see who was at my door. How the hell did she know where I lived?

Without hesitation I swung my front door open before realizing that I was only dressed in my underwear.

She suddenly flashed a sexy, white smile my way with breasts hanging out for me to salivate over. I was a mama's boy and she had breast fed, hence I was a titty man.

The tight, shorter than short jean shorts that she wore hugged her ass cheeks and made them literally ooze out of the bottom. Her camel toe was at full attention and I had to force myself to focus on her face.

"Tyson, happy birthday!" Climaxx yelled all excited like she and I were best of friends.

My eyes must've asked her what she was doing at my door because she told me, "Your boo sent me over. What's her name?"

I thought about it and then smiled. "Ari." *She* must've been my surprise.

What was my lady up to? Was she trying to test me?

"Yeah, your chick's cool as fuck. I'm tellin' you. She must be mighty secure sending me over here. Hmm. I'm just sayin', she told me that she's out of town and can't be here to…give you some birthday sex. I mean, not that I am gonna give you some, but I guess a lap dance is the next best thing judging by how you almost nutted all over yourself the last time I saw you." As she laughed she threw her long weave over her shoulder.

My eyes were all over her brick house frame and my mind was roaming. Still, I was Ari's man and I wasn't going to fuck that up. As far as I knew that bitch was going to report every detail of the night to her.

"Uh, I'm good shawty. As a matter of fact I was about to go to bed. My girl is a trip." I tried to laugh it off and throw a hint that I didn't need a lap dance for my birthday. "I'm with somebody yo' and I don't do this type of shit. It was fun that night at the club, but I can't do anything like this without my girl around."

"She told me that you were expecting a threesome with me that night." She let out a sneaky little laugh as she put her bag on the coffee table. "Relax. I ain't gonna bite you. I was sent to do a job and I'm a professional, so I'm gonna do it."

Her eyes roamed the room and then settled on my iHome speakers that sat on a shelf in the corner of the room.

"Perfect," she said as she walked over to it. My iPod Touch was mounted and ready to play.

That was due to the fact that I always wanted mood music playing when Ari was around. It wasn't for a lap dance from a sexy ass stripper that I was tempted to cheat on her with. What the fuck was going on? I just wished she'd get the lap dance over with so she could go. I was going to call Ari and let her know that wasn't the birthday present that I was expecting, nor did I want it. I mean, I did, but I didn't. Damn that bitch was sexy as fuck. I had to adjust my hard on so that I could sit comfortably.

Climaxx bent over in front of me as she searched for the perfect song. My eyes were glued to her plump ass cheeks. When she glanced back and licked her lips, I thought about paying her a little extra to suck my dick. All I had to do was ask her not to tell Ari. Besides, it was business and from what I could see, old girl was about her paper.

"You got something to drink and I don't mean no water or juice. Something nice and strong. Bring us both a drink. You need to loosen up." Her attention was back on the iPod and I reluctantly got up to fulfill her request.

Alcohol, a hard dick and a sexy, thick woman in my

house was a bad mix. I cursed Ari in my head. Why the fuck was she putting me in that position? As I poured Grey Goose into two glasses full of crushed ice, I promised myself that I wouldn't cheat on my girl. I would just let Climaxx gyrate all over my dick and then jack off when she left with thoughts of my girl's sweet pussy on my mind.

"Yeah, I can do this. Mind over matter," I said out loud as I added cranberry juice to the liquor.

When I returned to the room Climaxx had stripped down to a white, silky lingerie set. The six inch red stiletto heels that she wore had her tall, thick frame on beast mode. Fuck! I needed her out of my crib pronto. The song that was playing was Ciara's "Body Party" and it wasn't making it any easier to focus on fidelity.

"Here you go," I said as I passed her the drink, trying my hardest not to focus on the temptation in front of me.

"You can look Tyson. Your girl paid for you to look and enjoy." She took a sip of her drink and then placed it on a coaster on the glass coffee table beside her purse.

I put my drink down beside it and sat down. "Honestly, I don't think this is a good idea."

She sauntered over to me with her melon sized breasts jiggling. My eyes drifted down to her thighs and the V shaped treasure that sat between them. My mouth watered at the thought of those thighs wrapped around my waist as I pounded that pussy out. The old me was screaming to come out and play, but I fought to keep him at bay.

She put her finger to my lips. "It's okay. You're a big boy. You can keep your dick in your pants while I tease you. Your woman will be back soon, so use that pent up aggression on her. I'm sure she'll appreciate that."

I nodded, mesmerized by the beautiful Amazon. If I was a single man I'd let her do whatever she wanted to do to me, but I wasn't and she was just there for a lap dance. She took a large gulp of her drink and put it down again.

"You scared to get tipsy around me? Don't trust yourself?" She asked as she turned and started twerking that ass in front of me.

My dick throbbed as she backed it up and started gyrating in circles on my lap. She reached back and rubbed the top of my head with her soft hands as she worked that ass on me. I couldn't stop watching her ass cheeks clap in that thong and was waiting for her to take it off so that I could see that pretty pussy again. If Ari wanted me to enjoy, that was what I planned to do.

When the song went off Climaxx stood and turned to face me.

"Okay, you get one more song and this time it's your choice." Her juicy lips were glossy and inviting. Oh how I wanted them wrapped around my dick.

What was a birthday without an orgasm? Damnit. That was probably my first birthday without getting any since I was eighteen. My girl sure did have some making up to do. Shit. Not only was she not there to relieve my sexual tension, but she'd sent a bitch I'd love to fuck to tease me. The nerve of her. My second thought was to fuck Climaxx's fine ass just to get at her. That's what the fuck she would've deserved.

"I think I've had enough," I said instead.

Climaxx smiled at me and shook her head. "Nope. Your girl paid top dollar, so you're gonna get what she paid for."

As I shook my head, I sighed in frustration. That bitch wanted me to fuck her. Something told me to call Ari, but I'd play her game right along with her. I got up and made my way over to the iPod. As I strolled through the music choices I found Ludacris's "Pussy Poppin'." Fuck all that lovey dovey music. It was what it was. She was a stripper and she was getting paid to give me a private show. Well, then let's get it popping.

I made my way back over to her and she passed me my drink. "Go ahead and drink a little bit. You might as well relax and get into it. From what your girl tells me, you two are on your way to the alter. You might as well enjoy this while you can."

A smile fought its way through my serious glare. "For real? She said that?"

Climaxx drained her glass and smiled back at me. "Hell yeah."

I gulped my drink down and felt my body relax immediately. When I sat down that time, I decided to go ahead and get into it. Hey, she was there for me, so I was going to take full advantage of her sexy body. Well, not physically, just visually.

After a minute or so of her putting her ass and pussy in my face, she was butt naked. I was allowed to touch, so I did, starting with those big ass titties. Fighting the desire to put one of her nipples in my mouth, I suddenly felt light headed as hell. Damn, what the fuck was going on? All I'd had were a couple beers with my pops and a little vodka.

"Uhhh….damn…mmm…"

The sound of moans seemed far away and my body felt tingly as hell, but I couldn't really move or speak. I could feel hands on me, but I felt disoriented, like it was a dream. When I finally opened my eyes, my vision was blurry. It looked like Climaxx was on my lap, moving up and down. She threw her head back as her fingers danced all over my chest.

"Mmm...Ty...shit..."

All of a sudden all I saw was black.

Chapter 10

Ari

"Hello?" I'd just left the post office sending off very special packages and was annoyed by the ringing of my cell phone. I was on my way to the formal shop in order to find a sexy and borderline revealing dress that would be sure to make Tyson shit himself when he saw me. I was ready to get this entire adventure over with so that I could move. Judging by the unfamiliar number showing up on my CALLER ID I assumed that something or someone was about to disrupt my flow.

"Ari? It's me Ren." Her voice sounded so distraught which only irritated me further. Clearly she had a problem. The fact that she was calling indicated that I must have overly sold her the idea that I gave a fuck.

"Okay?" I got off of the exit for the mall and half-assed listened to whatever she had to say.

"Tyson filed an assault charge against me and a restraining order."

"Mmhmmm." This wasn't new information. Tyson had already informed me of his response to her antics.

"When I came home yesterday the damn police were waiting for me! Waiting for me! They took my baby from me, Ari. I'm here at the Dekalb County Jail and they're holding me for $2000.00 bail. I don't have $2000.00!"

I was wondering why any of that was my problem. My silence propelled her to keep speaking with more urgency.

"I need your help!" She cried out. "I only did what you told me to do, what you paid me to do, and now I'm in fuckin' jail. The whole point of me doing this was to get the extra money that I needed to take care of my kid. You got me into this--"

I had to stop her right there. "I got you into this?" I questioned. "No, sweetie. That's not exactly how that went down now is it? I paid you to distract him, to piss him off, and to hamper him from leaving home once. I never told you to hit his ass with a rock. I never told you to steal his phone. You did a lot of this extra shit on your own Ren. Besides, I gave you your other $5000.00 so if you pissed it away that's your problem, not mine."

"I didn't piss it away," she whined. "I used it to pay back payments on my car note and to cover some debts. I used it wisely. Now had I suspected that I was going to be arrested I would have saved a little more to bail my own ass out of jail."

Was she getting slick with me? I switched lanes so that I could prepare to get off at my exit. "So what do you want from me now?"

"You're the only person I know with the cash to get me out of here. Please, if we hadn't been on this whole revenge trip I wouldn't even be here."

There she was again, blaming me for her own fallacies.

I sighed. "Fine, Ren. Fine. I'll be down there in about an hour with the money."

"Thank you!" She gushed. "Oh my God. You're the best. Thank you so much.

I'll pay you back somehow. I swear whatever you need me to do."

The offer sounded promising but I knew better. If Ren could afford to pay anyone anything she wouldn't have been so eager to jump at my original proposition. I turned into the entrance of the mall and felt a sense of urgency to get her off of my phone line.

"Okay hun. I'll be down there. Don't worry, okay. I'll see you soon." The lie rolled off of my tongue with ease.

I could hear her sobbing deeply over the phone. "Thank you, Ari. Thank you. I just needa get my kid back. This shit just got deeper than I ever intended. But I know you…I know you can help me fix this, right? Help me turn it around."

I stopped the car and stared out of the windshield. Was she kidding? She really believed that I was her guardian angel or something. "Okay, Ren. Keep it together. Be there soon." I hung up before she could utter another pathetic word.

I slipped my phone into my purse and exited my car. I had a dress to buy. I didn't have time to be fixing someone else's mistakes. Besides, my special account for this project was dwindling. I couldn't bear to spend another unnecessary dime towards its execution. No remorse filled my heart as I ventured towards the formal wear shop. I had a reunion to get ready for.

***

"So, will we be running into a lot of your old girlfriends?" I asked Tyson as we walked hand and hand through the outdoor Farmer's Market.

It was the weekend before the class reunion and we were spending the entire day together. We hadn't had much time together since his birthday. Time simply hadn't permitted it with all of my planning and other things I had to tend to. Tyson had been getting antsy, no doubt he was incredibly horny. He'd mentioned his birthday present to me only once and I figured that sending Climaxx over to entice him had gone better than he really wanted to admit to me.

Unable to put him off any longer, I'd agreed to spend the day with him. First we were shopping for the ingredients for an authentic Caribbean dish that he claimed he was skilled at making. Since the outdoor market was relatively close to my home and

I'd yet to ever invite Tyson over, I figured today was as good a time as any to show him around my personal space. The truth was that I didn't intend to stay there much longer anyway, so I didn't see the harm in letting my man know where I lived, especially since we'd come so far.

"No," Tyson answered, gripping my hand tighter. "I didn't have many girlfriends in high school."

I shot him a stunned look. "What? Are you serious? You strike me as the kind of guy who would be prom king and homecoming king. You know, one of those popular, pretty boy types."

He chuckled. "Okay, okay...I was homecoming king but--"

"Wow," I cut in, laughing and shaking my head. "I knew it. You were that guy, huh? I bet all the little cheerleaders couldn't wait to shake their pom poms at you could they?"

"Come on, give a brother a break. I couldn't help that I was popular. It wasn't like I asked for the popularity or anything. You know, it just happened. I was just...I don't know...me."

"And, the homecoming queen?" I asked. "Was she your girlfriend?"

"Naw, not really."

"No and not really are two different things," I snapped. "Either she was or she wasn't."

It was now Tyson's turn to look at me with a shocked expression. "Is someone getting a little jealous?"

I shot him a deadly look and quickly looked away. His question damn near made me want to say something that I knew would not have been a good look.

"It's all in the past Ari," he said, pulling me to him and kissing me on the nose. "It's all in the past. You are my present and my future beautiful. I plan to make you happy for my days and years to come."

I smiled and pulled away from him. "I'm going to go get some mangos okay?"

"Hurry back to me," he said looking as if he didn't want me to go.

I walked in the opposite direction and took my time perusing the fruit. I liked mangos, but I'd really used getting them as an excuse to have a moment away from Tyson. Being with him affected me in a way that I didn't really expect that it would. Talking about his high school days really took me to another place-- a place I didn't really care to visit.

Calm down, Ari, I mentally chided myself. *Calm down, girl. You're almost to the finish line. Everything is going to be okay. You can do this.* I grabbed my mangos, took a deep breath, and turned around to rejoin my boyfriend near the vegetables. I was engrossed in looking at the different array of fruits, some of which I hadn't even heard of, and even considered trying something new. In the distance I could see Tyson as he stopped and began to speak to someone that appeared oddly familiar.

"What the hell," I said out loud. Quickly, I dodged behind a Noni Juice display and peered over a row of bottles. I was close enough to hear their conversation.

"Sister Smith?" Tyson called out in a surprised fashion as he looked at the older woman. "Wow, it's been years."

The woman looked at him with a peculiar expression. She was trying to place him. I squinted and watched as recognition hit her. "Tyson Reid," she mouthed. A look of disdain fluttered across her face followed by indifference which settled upon her sullen eyes and turned up her lips. "Been quite some time."

"It has, it has," Tyson stated. "Um…how've you been?"

"Been well as can be expected considering some things. Yourself?"

"Been great actually. Life has really been kind to me, especially here lately."

She nodded her head. "Our Lord is a merciful God."

Tyson's body expression suggested that he felt awkward and was trying to figure out how to walk away from her without being rude. "Yes…yes he is. He's certainly blessed me."

"I can only hope that repentance played a great role in the receipt of those blessings."

I pursed my lips and wondered how Tyson would respond to the shot that had obviously been taken at him.

"Um…I can't tell you have sorry I am for what happened back then, Ms. Smith," Tyson stated.

My ears were wide open.

"I mean, we were all kids back then and while hindsight is twenty-twenty, I still feel really sorry for any heartache I caused the both of you." Tyson held his arms out and in one hand was his cell phone. "I mean, I wish there was something I could do to take it all back but I can't…all I can do is say I'm sorry."

The woman's eyes trailed from Tyson's lips to his extended right hand and the phone that lingered there. She pointed to it. "Is that…is it…?" Her question wouldn't quite come out the way she wanted it to.

I couldn't see what it was that was on the screen of Tyson's phone and I damn near knocked over the Noni Juice display trying to get another look in vain.

Tyson followed the woman's glance and held the phone closer to her for her to get a better view. "This picture? Oh, that's my girlfriend."

The woman was confused. "My, that's my…" Again her words trailed off.

Tyson frowned. "Your who?"

"You're together now?" The woman asked in a bewildered tone. "My…" I couldn't hear her words as her thoughts began to come out in fragments.

Sounding very assertive, Tyson shut down whatever conclusions the woman had jumped to. "No, Ms. Smith. This is my girlfriend, Ari."

The woman frowned. Obviously, she wasn't convinced.

Tyson placed his phone in his pocket and reached out to touch the woman's arm. "Ms. Smith, when was the last time you talked to her?"

Her, I wondered. Were they really going to sit here and continue going down memory lane as if either or both of them expected to reconnect all parties involved?

"Years," Ms. Smith answered. "It's been years. I want to change that, but…" She hesitated for a minute. "And you?"

"Not at all," Tyson answered. "And honestly, I think it might be best for everyone if we just leave the past in the past. Any chance that she'll be attending the reunion?"

Ms. Smith shook her head. "No. I doubt it." She sighed. "It's understandable though. I wouldn't want to relive any of the past either if I were her."

Tyson nodded. "Yeah…understandable. If you speak to her let her know that I'm really sorry and that I pray that life has been good to her."

The woman nodded, still looking confused. "Yes. Prayer is good so long as it's done with a sincere heart."

Tyson nodded. "Take care, ma'am."

"You too, son." She walked away with her back to me as Tyson pulled out his phone.

I took a few minutes to make sure that the woman was completely out of view before I walked over to Tyson. I intended to pull him away in the opposition direction. I tapped him on the shoulder and he looked up at me with a dazed expression.

"Everything okay?" I asked sweetly, wondering if he'd tell me what the hell had just gone down.

He looked down at the photo on his cell and then back up at me without saying a word. His eyes narrowed in as he studied my face in silence.

"What?" I asked feeling a little self-conscious.

"I uh…I just noticed how some of your facial expressions kinda um…kinda remind me of someone I used to know," he told me.

"Oh? Is that good or bad?"

He returned the phone to his pocket once more and tried to shrug off whatever was plaguing him. "Neutral I guess. You know…it was just someone from the past."

I placed my arm through his and looked up at him adoringly. "An old girlfriend huh? One of those chicks I'm gonna meet at the reunion?"

He kissed my nose. "Naw, nothing like that. And no one you have to be concerned with. Just a mistake from the past."

I cringed. "I remind you of a mistake? Damn, I don't know which is worse…you thinking of some female as a mistake, I mean that's cold-hearted, or you feeling as if I remind you of a mistake."

He pulled me close. "Don't think much into it, Ari. Seriously. When I look at you baby all I think about is how much I love you."

I nearly fainted. He'd never said those words to me before. I mean, I'd suspected that I'd gotten him hooked with no chance of turning back. But, he hadn't vocalized this exact sentiment until that very moment and I was surprised by the way the words sounded as they rolled off of his tongue. "Excuse me?" I whispered.

Tyson grabbed both of my hands and stared into my eyes. There we were standing in the middle of the Farmer's Market with strangers walking by watching the moment that I'd kind of envisioned going down another, more romantic way. But, I couldn't stop it or change it, nor did I want to. I wanted to hear him profess his true emotions because no matter where we were when it happened, I knew that it would be a memory we'd both remember for the rest of our lives.

"Ever since you came into my life I have felt so complete...so mesmerized by everything about you," Tyson explained. "I can't wait to see your beautiful face every day. Everything makes me think about you. I find myself imagining stuff about my future and you're always in the equation. It's taken a lot for me to get to the point where I'm ready to commit and settle down. In all honesty, you make me want to be the best man possible, Ari. You make me want to be that man for you and I love you for that."

I smiled at him and felt my heart actually flutter. He was so sincere and the words were so heartfelt. I wondered how many times he'd given similar speeches with less enthusiasm. I knew what he was saying to me was the real deal because of the way his eyes glistened as he spoke and the way he gripped my hands as if he was holding on tight for extra support.

"You sound like a man that's serious about what he wants," I said softly.

"Definitely. I want to spend my life with you," he replied.

"Is this an impromptu proposal?" I asked giving him the side eye.

"Naw, I know better than that. You're worth too much and you're way too special to me to just give you an out of the blue, unplanned, unromantic proposal with no ring. You deserve better than that."

I smiled as he leaned in and kissed me tenderly on the lips.

"When I propose it's going to be a memorable, Ari-rated occasion," he said softly with confidence.

"Is that right?" I teased.

"That's right. You just be ready to say yes."

"Trust me, my response is going to change your life." I reached my arms around him and pulled his neck down to kiss him once more with my lips purposely closed. Tyson tried to French kiss me, but I broke the embrace without letting his tongue part my lips. "Come on. Let's get out of here."

He simply nodded. We walked off hand in hand carrying our selected items for purchase. While Tyson was most likely envisioning wedding bells, I was envisioning the inferno of the emotions to come. Yes, our future was about to be solidified very soon.

Chapter 11

Ari

My red cocktail dress was the truth. The plunging neckline was daring and the fabric of the knee length dress clung to my curves just right. My locks were pulled up into a neat ponytail of curly tresses and long tear drop diamond earrings hung from my lobes. A platinum necklace with a clustered diamond pendant rested alluringly within the swell of my breasts. My six inch open toe stilettos were blinged out with sparkly rhinestones. I was literally shining with radiance from head to toe. Tonight was sure to be epic.

Tyson could barely keep his eyes off of me as we made our way through the Fox Theatre for the Carver High School class of

2005's ten year reunion. Music blared, couples entered the doors dressed in their best, and memories flooded through the entire atmosphere. Tyson's popularity was made apparent by the way people continued to come up to him enthusiastically and I couldn't help but notice the way that some of the women glared at him from their respectable distances across the room. I kept my eyes averted at times when I felt that their stares were penetrating my eyes as if trying to tap into my soul. Shaking off the feelings that began to cloud my judgment I turned my back to the majority of the crowd and half-assed listened as Tyson chopped it up with one of his oldest friends.

"Shitttt, my nigga, my nigga," Tyson's homeboy stated. "You needa stay in touch with ya' boy! Man, I remember all the shit we used to get into. Dem was some wild days."

Tyson laughed. "Shit yeah!" He looked over at me and smiled. "Aye, Manny, this is the love of my life, Ari Smit."

I smiled politely and reached out to shake Manny's hand. His eyes never left the risqué amount of skin that I was showing.

"Love of your life huh?" Manny questioned. "Mmm-mmm. You did good for yourself, homie. With a fine ass woman like this I would never leave the house bruh."

Tyson put an arm around me possessively. "If we never left the house then jealous brothers like you wouldn't be able to kick yourself 'cause you ain't got what I got."

Manny laughed. "Aight, aight." He looked over and caught two women glancing in our direction. "Don't forget to mention the jealous chicks who all thought that they were going to become Mrs. Tyson Reid back in the day."

Tyson waved his friend off. "Man, go on with that."

"Ari, lemme tell you, ya' man over here used to be the lady-killer of our class. Had the girls slinging mud at each other trying to get up with him."

"She doesn't want to hear all that talk man," Tyson insisted.

I lovingly placed a hand on his chest and smiled flirtatiously at Manny. "No, no, no! Dish it 'cause tight lips over here won't give me the real about his game back in the day."

"Oh, my bruh had much game," Manny confirmed. "Much game. He ain't keep a chick longer than a couple of weeks with the way they flocked to him." Manny hit Tyson's arm. "Aye, remember that bet first semester senior year?"

My eyes sparkled. It was clear that dirt was about to be exposed. "What bet?"

"Leave the past in the past, man," Tyson stated. "We've all moved on."

"Shhhh," I whispered, hushing him up. "Spill it!" My eyes never left Manny.

Manny laughed. "Yeah, it's the past, bruh. No harm, no foul. Ari, ya' boy took this bet with the other members of the basketball team, right. He was starting that year as point guard and it was kinda like a hazing thing. Anyway, we bet him that he couldn't hit the weirdest girl in our class. This scrawny, quiet chick whose moms had her wearing long skirts all the time…going

234

to church damn near every day of the week.
She ain't never do nothing. No school
activities, didn't hang with nobody. Her
moms acted like everybody was the devil.
I'm talkin' chick had bad acne. No sex
appeal at all."

"You act like the girl was all tore up,"
Tyson stated. "She wasn't *that* bad."

"Shhhiiiit," Manny replied. "That girl
couldn't get it with another nigga's dick."

I gave a tight-lipped smile. "My, oh
my. Who won the bet?" I looked from
Tyson to Manny to see who was going to
give me the scoop.

"Ya' boy went in," Manny stated. "I
couldn't believe that he had ole girl thinking
that he actually liked her. I mean she was all
in."

"Yeah, yeah," I interrupted. "But did he hit it?"

"This fool hit that thang and had ole girl turned out. The whole school was clowning when Tyson told her during half time at one of our games that he wasn't feeling her ass. Gave her the boot in front of everybody." Manny laughed. "She'd made some poster for him and had walked onto the court to give him a kiss like they were a real couple. Yearbook committee was snapping pics galore. You shoulda seen her face. Ole girl ran off the court crying while the whole school went crazy. We heard she went crazy or some shit, didn't even come back to school after that. She just dropped out. Then word on the street was that this dummy went and knocked her ass up."

I looked to Tyson immediately for confirmation.

Tyson was mortified. "That was a rumor. We don't know that she was pregnant for real."

"Her home-girl Deb said it," Manny countered. "That was her only friend so I believe it. Plus her moms seemed to get extra weird after that. Shooing folks away when they came near her building. Throwing holy water at us. Speaking nonsense like she was praying over us or something."

"Still," Tyson said. His discomfort was obvious. "We don't know for sure and I sure ain't paying nobody no child support so..."

"Yeah, Deb was like her moms sent her away so ain't no telling what happened to your seed," Manny argued.

"Man, let it go," Tyson said, giving his friend a stern look.

Manny was ready to drop it. He took a glass of champagne from a server who was walking by and began to move his body to the rhythm of the Mario ballad that was playing. "Anyway, you gotta make some time to come up to North Carolina and get at me sometime, Ty. Time to get out of Atlanta and see something different bruh."

"Yeah, I do," Tyson stated. "But I gotta make sure to come when you between wives. You know how you get when you're booed up."

"You one to talk obviously," Manny joked, taking another look at me. "But yeah, now would be a good time to make plans 'cause my divorce was finalized two months ago."

The men shared a laugh as my eyes ventured over to a man and woman who were heading our way. The man had a determined expression while his woman looked a little pensive. I could only imagine what was going on. Before they could come within ear shot I was dying to know something. "How much was the bet for?" I asked Manny and Tyson.

"What?" Tyson asked, focusing in on me.

"The bet," I repeated. "When you slept with the ugly girl. You know, the school joke. How much was the bet?"

"Oh, it wasn't nothing," Manny offered. "The rest of us had to cover his senior fees and prom shit. This dude was the flyest nigga at the prom."

I was floored. He'd initiated all that ridicule and heartbreak just for the sake of saving a few hundred dollars on his end of the year shit? I couldn't decide if he was a shallow motherfucker, or just a horrible ass dude. Maybe it was a little bit of both, but as I stared at him I had to fight the urge to take Manny's drink out of his hand and pour it in Tyson's face.

"Tyson Reid!" Another male voice boomed out over the sound of Usher's 'Confessions'.

We all faced the angry, muscular man who stood toe to toe with Tyson while the woman with him stood just behind him.

"Brandon Phelps," Tyson stated. "What's good, man?"

"You tell me," Brandon spat back.

Tyson shrugged. "Not much going on here man. Long time no see."

"Yeah, but my wife's seen you a lot more recently than I have."

My eyebrows went up.

Tyson took a step back as my eyes burned holes in the side of his head. "Come again?"

"You remember my wife Kristi."

I looked over to Kristi who gave me a scrutinizing look in return. Instantly I turned my body away and averted my eyes. I didn't need whatever drama she may have felt inclined to hurl my way.

Tyson looked over Brandon's shoulder and nodded. "I mean, of course. How you doing, Kristi?"

"I was doing fine until your little antics, Tyson," Kristi stated.

Tyson shook his head. "Look, I'm not sure what either of you are talking 'bout but I--"

"Give it to me, Kristi!" Brandon demanded, holding his hand out to his wife.

Kristi pulled a four by six snapshot from her purse and handed it to her husband with a frown.

"This shit was not cool nigga," Brandon said to Tyson. "Next time you wanna send ya' fuckin' Johnson to someone be sure to leave my wife off ya' list!" He pressed the picture into Tyson's chest.

"What the hell?" Tyson commented as he grabbed it and looked down at the photo. His eyes bulged and he swallowed hard. "Man…Brandon, I didn't send this to Kristi."

"No?" Brandon challenged. "You telling me that ain't yo dick?"

Silence seemed to come over the auditorium as some of Tyson's classmates closed in around the scenario.

"I mean…I mean…" Tyson couldn't deny it. He knew his own dick, but admitting to the former linebacker that it was definitely his member just wasn't something he felt comfortable doing in front of his entire graduating class. He lowered his head staring at the photo before taking a quick glance at me with my arms folded.

"That's what I thought," Brandon retorted.

"I mean, what we had was a long time ago," Kristi said. "So I'm not sure what made you think it was okay to come at me like this."

"I'm telling you I didn't send this to you!" Tyson's voice was escalated.

"Don't yell at my wife!" Brandon said threateningly. "We know you sent this shit 'cause it came addressed from you with ya' lil' note about always wanting to share a special part of you. I'm telling you homeboy, you real close to getting ya' foul ass dealt with."

I could see the sweat beads forming along the side of Tyson's temple. He was in some deep shit and I could tell that the reunion wasn't turning out the way he'd expected.

"Look, Brandon," he said, trying to remain rational. "I understand your frustration, but I wouldn't do no shit like this man. Where would I even get your address from? That shit with Kristi was a long, long time ago. I'm not living for some high school shit. As you can see, I got the finest woman in the world by my side," he said motioning to me. "No disrespect to you Kristi, but I don't have a need to be on some foul shit trying to rehash some old flame. This is our ten year reunion man. Not homecoming."

"Then you shouldn't be doing teen-aged boy shit like showing off your dick," Kristi shot back, feeling slighted anyway.

"I told you I didn't send this to you!" Tyson snapped. "You ain't got nothing I want and I wouldn't be tryin' to get it up for you in person, or to send no damn pic."

"I told you 'bout yelling at my wife you perv," Brandon let out before suddenly cocking back and landing a punch against Tyson's nose.

Blood dripped on impact and the crowd went wild from the unexpected turn of events. Tyson touched his nose, but couldn't catch the crimson that stained the front of his white button up Gucci dress shirt. He stepped forward with his right fist in mid-air and the small photo in his left hand.

Manny jumped between Tyson and Brandon in an effort to diffuse any more violence. "Hold up, hold up! Naw, we're not doing this here. We all grown. Y'all better talk this out like men."

"You put ya' hands on the wrong one homeboy," Tyson said menacingly to Brandon over Manny's shoulder as he reached into the pocket of his tux jacket and pulled out the silk handkerchief.

"And you done pushed up on the wrong nigga's wife," Brandon replied.

"And I keep telling yo' ass that I didn't send that shit," Tyson said between clenched teeth.

"That's bullshit," some high-pitched voice erupted from the front of the ensuing crowd. "I don't know how much pussy you think you need, but you sure as hell are on the prowl 'cause I got ya' special dick pic too."

I looked the woman up and down and shook my head at her $50 little black dress thinking that she could have tried a little harder to achieve the look of class that I assumed she was going for.

"Me too," another woman chimed in.

"Yeah, I got that same picture," a dark skinned beauty admitted. "And here I thought I was special. My dumb ass was all set to give you a little something in return." She looked at me and rolled her eyes. "Until I saw you roll up in here with your Barbie Doll."

I laughed out loud though the rest of the crowd found nothing funny about the scandal plaguing their reunion. I found it amusing that this chick was so blatant with her jealousy. It didn't faze me one bit. I was used to the haterism and ridicule. Some women just couldn't appreciate the beauty of another woman. Immediately she became instantly unattractive to me. To me, inner beauty trumped any amount of outer beauty that anyone could be blessed with. It was just too bad that I'd encountered so many inwardly ugly individuals.

"Aye, watch ya' self," Tyson warned the dark-skinned chick with his hand held up to her. "Now listen y'all…it seems most of you got this indecent picture and I swear I would have never sent this out. I don't know who…" He stopped talking and kind of stared into thin air as he processed whatever it was that was running through his mind. He held his head down a little and laughed while looking at the portrait of his member. "Wow," he said. "A'ight, I've been harassed lately by an ex who has stopped at nothing to ruin my life. Clearly, this was another one of her attempts to get even with me for leaving her."

I shook my head at him. He needed to know that it was clear to me that he'd been holding out on some information.

"So, you just that damn irresistible that women going stupid trying to embarrass you for not wanting them?" A female asked in disgust. "Some things never change."

"Aye, y'all know good and well how you females get over Ty," Manny stated coming to Tyson's defense. "Don't get brand new."

"It's time for him and the women he mess with to grow up," the woman suggested, rolling her eyes and walking away.

"I'm sorry for the pics ladies," Tyson said to the crowd of angry, disappointed, and annoyed women. "I'm truly sorry. I never meant for this to happen and I hate that your evening was ruined because of this nonsense."

"A'ight, break it up! Break it up," Manny called out just as the hired security for the evening came over to check the commotion of the crowd.

Tyson's classmates began to disperse and Tyson threw the image of his dick into a nearby trashcan as he held his handkerchief to his nose. I almost felt sorry for him, but with all that I'd heard I felt he deserved a little retro payback.

"I'm sorry, Ari," he said apologetically. "I woulda never brought you here if I knew any of this was gon' go down."

"I guess that I actually did end up encountering some of your exes huh?" I retorted.

He shook his head. "It's not like that."

"And your crazy ex…the one that knocked the shit out of you with the rock…that's who you think is responsible for this fiasco here tonight?"

He nodded. "I'm sure of it. Crazy bitch."

"Sounds like she's been continuously on one beyond the rock incident." I looked at him, daring him to lie to me again.

Tyson sighed. "Babe, as much as I really don't wanna keep nothing from you I just really, really can't get into this with you tonight. Not right now, babe."

My nostrils were flaring, my body temperature was rising, and my temples were pounding. That moment was pushing me to my own breaking point. It was time to exit stage left before I ruined everything by acting out of instant emotion. I looked up and noticed a group of women in a hurdle still throwing dirty looks my way. Yeah, it was definitely time to go. I'd seen and heard quite enough.

"Maybe we should get out of here," I told Tyson.

He nodded. "Definitely."

I followed him past the group of shade throwing females as we headed for the exit.

"I could have sworn it was her," one of them whispered.

"Mmmhmmm, not looking like that," another one replied

"I don't know," the ring leader came back. "He coulda took his ugly duckling nerd and turned her into a beautiful swan."

The other women chuckled.

"Shit, she ain't all that," one of the other women stated. "If he wanted a dime he coulda got with me."

"Hmmm," the last one chimed in. "If he was sticking his dick in ole' girl back then ain't no telling who he'd stick it in now. Tyson obviously has no standards. You don't want that dick in your girl. Ain't no telling what he walkin' 'round with."

Listening to their banter as we tried to escape the pits of reunion hell made me want to turn around and give them all the business. Who were they to be talking about who Tyson's dick was running up in when they were obviously foaming at the mouth over the possibility of getting dicked down by him? They were making it seem as if him getting with the unpopular chick from back in the day was such a travesty. The bigoted, judgmental, demeaning mindset of that group of people really got up under my skin. My emotions were raging and I didn't think I could step foot on the pavement outside without losing control.

"I'm going to the ladies' room," I announced to Tyson's retreating figure abruptly.

He stopped and looked back at me. "A'ight," he replied in a huff. "I'll be outside. I need some air."

And I needed a moment so I walked off without responding to his statement. Luckily, the rest room was empty when I entered. I started to lock the door to keep anyone else from coming in, but I didn't do it. Instead, I walked over to one of the sinks and stared at my reflection in the mirror. The eyes glaring back at me where woeful and pleading. They were asking me to make it right. I gripped the sink with both hands, pulled back as I leaned downward, and let out an anguished cry. I howled as if I was at home in the privacy of my own bathroom, unable to contain myself.

"Aretha?"

I hadn't heard the gentle opening and closing of the restroom door. I also hadn't heard the woman's demure heels clicking against the granite of the lavish restroom floor as she approached me. But, as she spoke her one and only word while lightly touching my right arm, I flinched. I looked into her eyes and couldn't fight the connection that lingered between us. I considered giving in to it, but I knew it couldn't be done. I just couldn't do it.

"Excuse me?" I asked, jerking my arm away.

"I watched you for the longest," she stated. "I thought I was tripping, but the more I watched, the more I knew. You look amazing!"

I took in the kindness of her eyes, the sincerity of her smile, and the welcoming sensation that her aura provided to me. But still, she didn't know me and I wasn't about to get into any discussions about it. I shook my head, turned away, and pulled a few paper towels from the dispenser to my right.

"I'm sorry," I said. "You must have me confused with someone else."

"Aretha, it's me," she said. "Debbie. I know we haven't spoken in years, but I'd know you anywhere, girl. You don't have to front with me."

I wet the paper towels and dabbed at my face and neck with it in an attempt to cool off. "My name's Ari and I wasn't a member of your class," I told her. "I'm from Florida."

Debbie ignored me. "How's your mother? How are you? I really wish you'd reach out to me sometime. I miss you."

I looked at myself in the mirror once more and had to turn away from the reflection of the disturbed young woman looking back at me. Tossing the paper towels away, I faced the woman. "Sweetie, you're not listening to me. I'm not your friend. I'm sorry." I turned away and headed for the door.

"But I was always your friend," she said behind me. "And if you ever need to reach out to someone I can still be that friend…when you're done pretending."

I shook my head once more. Tyson's classmates were just too much. My breathing was irregular and I couldn't control it. Like Tyson, I needed some fresh air. I needed to be away from this stifling environment and these people that made me so angry and annoyed. For a bunch of adults they seemed to only have adult versions of their high school mentality. Now here was this nut trying to rebuild a friendship with a person that didn't exist. Unfortunately, Debbie didn't know me at all. I reached for the door and almost fell into a full blown panic attack when it didn't open for me.

"I locked it," Debbie informed me. "To give us some privacy."

Hmmm. Unfortunately, I hadn't heard her turn the lock upon entering either. I fumbled to unlock the door and pulled it open frantically. I had to get out. I had to get away. My chest was constricting. I hadn't signed up for this. No matter how much I tried to free myself, the anguish just wouldn't subside.

Chapter 12

Ari

2005

The humiliation I'd encountered at the hands of the guy I'd mentally and privately planned a happily ever after with wasn't enough. No, that searing pain that jolted through the crack in my already fragile heart just wasn't sufficient enough. To add insult to injury I was being forced into a life of silence and shame. I didn't want that. Would have never dared to wish it on my own worst enemy and there were plenty of people that had recently made it onto that list. But, it was happening and there was nothing I could do about it.

"No!!!" I screamed out, laid out on the floor in the modest living room of our one-story home holding on to the edge of the

sofa as if it was really sturdy enough to anchor me. "No! I don't wanna go! Please . don't make me go! Please don't do it!" My pleas were earnest and filled with sobs, but not of that was enough to move my mother and the evangelist that stood by her side in support.

"Get her up Miriam," Evangelist Norman instructed my mother with a stern face. "Get her up. You must hold the upper hand. That's exactly how she got herself into this predicament in the first place...no strong and hard rules. No parental enforcement of order, decorum, and the holy principles by which we are expected to live."

Mom tugged at my arms and with her shaky voice she tried to speak over my *crying. "Get up! Stop this. You have to go now. It's for the best."*

For the best? Was she kidding me? I shook my head defiantly and continued to hold on to the sofa with all of my might. "No! It's not right! It's not right!"

"You have to go! It's for the best. You'll see. Come on...please." Seeing that trying to convince me that this was indeed the right thing for us to do wasn't working, Mom began to beg me to comply. I was pretty sure that she only wanted to save face, what was left of it, in front of her peers...her spiritual leaders and greatest influences.

"Martin," Evangelista Norman called out to the Deacon standing in the doorway quietly watching the scene. She snapped her fingers and nodded in my direction.

"Don't make this harder than it already is," Mom told me. "You should want to go. You shouldn't want anyone to see you like this. I...I never wanted this for you. I wanted you to have better. You have to go now."

I looked up at her through the salty tears that were stinging my eyes. "Why would you do this to me? Why would you want to send me away? I'm your daughter! I'm your daughter!" As if the reminder was going to change the decision that the church had already made for her.

Mom looked over her shoulder at Evangelist Norman as the deacon reached down to grab me by my shoulders and pull me up to my feet like a little rag doll. Mom then looked back to me and said, "Any daughter of mine has got to know to respect her body. She's got to respect the Savior's teachings and not live in sin."

I couldn't believe it. There she stood justifying practically throwing me out into the street with her biblical reasoning. She actually believed that turning her back on me would make her more eligible to enter heaven on judgment day. As the deacon carried me to the door my eyes narrowed to thin slits as I stared my mother down. I saw her as weak and unloving. I saw her as possessed and brainwashed by what the people of the Greater Sense of Spirit Church of God in Christ were pouring into her head. This had nothing to do with uplifting and living God's words. Instead it had everything to do with image and how the church saw Mom, damn how it affected me and the rest of my life.

I could hear the rain as it beat down hard on the front porch behind me. The claps of thunder felt to me like God's angry roars at the injustice being done to one of his children in that moment. I would have said that to my mother then and there if I truly subscribed to all of the religious gibberish that she harped upon. The one thing that I knew for certain was that the basis of all religions was being a good person and treating others with kindness and respect. Where was the kindness here? Where was the respect? Where was the good that should have resided within my mother? Damn that, where was my mother because this monster was nothing more than the COGIC robot that her church leaders had turned her into.

"I hate you!" I spat out as I felt a tugging feeling within my abdomen. The pain was excruciating, but it was nothing like the hurt that I was experiencing emotionally. "I will never ever forgive you for this! What am I supposed to do? You're throwing me out into the street like trash."

"I'm not throwing you into the street," Mom retorted. "I'm saving you from yourself."

"Lies! You're ashamed of me! You're doing this for them. This isn't for me! I'm your daughter," I told her once more. "Your daughter! And you're discarding me…and your grandchild."

She lowered her eyes as if my saying it out loud stung her even more. That single action of disgrace and embarrassment let me know that no matter what she was lost to me forever. I no longer had a mother. I no longer had a family that was on my side no matter what. I didn't have the unconditional love that everyone yearned for. All I had was me, the embryo clinging to my womb, and a heart that was now shattered into a million pieces as I watched my mother literally turn away and put her back to me.

"I hate you!" I screamed. "You think you'll be blessed and favored for this? If anything you're going to the same hell that you've condemned me to!"

Evangelist Norman stepped forward as the Deacon pulled me across the threshold and into the pouring rain. "The word says that we are to honor our parents. Your disrespect of HIS commandments will no longer be tolerated. May you learn to respect yourself and turn into a halfway decent member of society." She closed the door to add a dramatic sense of finality to the scenario.

I cried and hollered as Martin nearly tossed me into the church's van. It didn't matter though. I knew that nobody was going to come to my rescue. My stomach was killing me. The cramps were damn near unbearable and I leaned over onto the torn seat cushion cradling my side as tears dripped down into my ears. I would have called my child's father the moment I'd arrived home earlier to find my mother packing my things. I would have asked him to come get me and help figure out what we were going to do, but that was impossible because he'd blocked my number from his home phone. Not only had he made it perfectly clear that he wanted nothing to do

*with me and had not liked me to begin with,
but he also wouldn't communicate with me.
I'd tried to call him before when I first found
out that I was pregnant, which was how I
learned that he'd blocked my number.
Confronting him in school was a no-go
because of the way he and his basketball
buddies and the rest of the popular crowd
would hoot and shun me the moment I came
into view. No, I was alone in the situation.
That was painfully clear.*

*About two hours outside of the
Atlanta city limits Martin made a stop to get
gas. I was not thrilled about going to the
group home for pregnant teens that my
mother was sending me to in the backwoods
of Macon, Georgia. I wasn't even being
allowed to graduate with my class, not that I
wanted to ever go back there and face the*

scrutinizing stares and snickers of my classmates. There was no future there for me at that group home. True, it was better than her sending me off to get an abortion, but then again that would have gone against her Christian principles. Still, I didn't want to live among a group of other shunned girls and be treated like some outcast. I wasn't a bad person, I didn't deserve to be exiled. From what I knew, those girls were forced to give their children up for adoption after giving birth. Why the hell would I go through all of that heartache just to hand over the person that had been growing within my body for nine months? I wasn't going to do it. I deserved better than that. My kid deserved a parent that wouldn't turn their back on them before he or she even saw the light of day.

As Martin stood at the counter inside of the gas station I made a split second decision. I wasn't going to let my mother or anyone else decide the course of my life. I opened the back door, slipped out of the van into the rain, and closed the door quickly. I took one look over toward the gas station and then hauled ass in the direction that we'd come from. I figured that was a better bet than going back in the direction we'd gone. I ran for my life and decided that I needed to get off of the main road just in case he decided to come looking for me. I ducked into the bushes, concealed by the darkness, the trees, and the heavy blankets of rain. I had no fear of what lied beneath the bushes. No wild animal or crazed person could be worse than all of the things I'd gone through already.

I don't know how long I ran or how far I'd gotten before stepping through the foliage and coming to another road. My feet couldn't go any longer. My body was in so much pain that I couldn't force it to cooperate with my mental longing to keep going. No lights appeared from any direction and I had no clue where I was. I had no money and no form of communication. I was out there in the middle of nowhere alone and growing woozier and woozier by the minute. I stopped to catch my breath and felt my body sink to the hard asphalt underneath me. The cramping in my sides was much worse now and I as I leaned over in agony I felt myself peeing through my jeans. As the liquid slowly permeated the inner thighs of my pant legs consciousness left me and all I

could see within my mental as my eyes
fluttered was the image of my mother's back.

***

A day later I found myself being
released from a hospital that I didn't even
remember being brought to. The discharge
nurse informed me that I'd been brought in
by some good Samaritans – a couple – and
that they'd found me passed out on the side
of the road. I felt it was a miracle that I
hadn't been run over by a car out there in
the middle of nowhere. The couple had been
passing through on their way to a vacation
spot and had left a name and number for me
to contact them. The nurse gave me the slip
of paper and I placed it in the pocket of my
jeans. Looking down at myself I realized
how horrible my appearance was. But what
rocked me were the brown stains on my

pants. I looked up to the nurse for some kind of explanation.

"You lost some blood before they brought you in," she stated, holding my discharge papers to her. "You've kind of been in and out since the procedure. I'm sure the doctors have talked to you about this, but I can go over it with you again if you'd like."

My expression was blank.
"Procedure?"

"When the couple brought you in you were miscarrying, honey. From an ectopic pregnancy. That's where the blood came from."

Instantly I touched my stomach.
"What?" I took stock of the way my body felt and realized that I did feel a tad lighter.

"I'm sorry. Your right fallopian tube busted from the growth of the pregnancy. The doctors had to remove the tube and the remnants of the fetal matter. The tube was already badly damaged from the untreated STD and then the scarring from the D&C doesn't help. The left tube, though not busted, is also badly damaged from the STD."

"STD?" I repeated.

"You tested positive for gonorrhea, honey. When left untreated like that it can really mess up your insides causing all kinds of pelvic infections."

The news was astonishing. My life just kept getting worse and worse. "Is it gone?" I asked. "The gonorrhea...isn't it curable?"

"We treated you for it, but you'll want to visit your GYN to follow up immediately.

Um…we didn't have anyone to contact for you so…"

I rose from the hospital bed. "I don't have family," I told her. "Anything else I need to know?" I was anxious to get away from the hospital so that I could digest all of the information I'd been hit with.

"Here's some literature about the condition, the ectopic pregnancy. And here's something else about the procedure you received and instructions for aftercare. Here's your prescription for the pain meds."

"I um…I don't have insurance or money."

The nurse looked at me. "Look, it's not my place to tell you what to do but you seem really young so take this for what it's worth. Go home. If you were running away because of the pregnancy just go home and talk to your folks. You're going to need to take it easy for a while and you need a support system. I'm sure if you just talk to your parents you can work through whatever issues you're having. This infection you suffered...this is going to change your life."

"Change my life?"

"You're sterile now, honey. When you get older and fall in love your chances of building a family are slim to none. That's not an easy thing to digest especially at your age. You need your family. Trust me on this."

I looked the woman in her eyes and felt a hardness occur. She assumed that I was some out of control, overly sexed, irresponsible teenager who was running away from home because she'd gotten knocked up. I wondered how her tone would be and what her advice would be if she knew that I'd actually been put out of my mother's home because she was ashamed of me. I wondered how sympathetic the woman would be if she knew that my dead child's father had impregnated me as a result of a joke, a stupid bet, which had in turn made me out to be the laughing stock of my school.

"Thanks for your help," I said to her as I made my way to the door.

"You need to stop by the financial counselor on the way out to discuss your hospital bill," she advised me as she followed me into the hall. She pointed to the office. "Just through that door."

I nodded. "Thank you. Where's the restroom?"

"Across the hall," she stated. "The counselor's waiting for you. I'll let her know you're in the restroom."

"Thanks," I replied curtly as I walked to the restroom. Once inside I shot into survival mode. I didn't have insurance or any kind of ID on me. My mother had stripped me of everything. I was completely on my own. There was no way that I was going to go into that financial counselor's office and have her call my mother to tell her anything that was going on. It was bad enough that she saw me as a failure; an unwed mother. But, if she learned that I was also diseased she would surely have a fit and would probably hang up the phone on me. I didn't need her to push me aside any more than she already had.

I looked around the restroom and did the only thing that I could think to do. I climbed up the wall using the trashcan to hold me up and shimmied out of the small window. Fuck their hospital bill, I needed to go out and figure out how I was going to survive.

***

And survive I did. I couldn't get a decent job anywhere without an ID and I didn't have any experience at anything anyway. After sleeping in doorways and public restrooms for a couple of days, I'd found a women's shelter where I was fortunate enough to secure room and board for a while. It was there that I met a woman who told me about how she was taking a break from her pimp so that she could rest her pussy for a while. Listening to her tell me about the money she made fucking this dude and that turned my stomach at first, but after a while it began to sound like an easy way to make my own money so that I could somehow afford to do something else with my life. So, when Bambi decided to go back to Red Roc, her pimp, she carried me along with her.

Red Roc was more than happy to put my ass on the stroll, but the impression that Bambi had given me of the setup was nothing like the reality. I didn't realize just how many men would be violating my body on a nightly basis, or that Red Roc would pocket most of my money not giving a damn about my plans to save. I spent my eighteenth birthday being fucked by a group of rowdy hood niggas who had managed to secure a lavish hotel suite, most likely with their drug dealing earnings, and was having a going away party for one of their homeboys who had decided to join the military. Their mode of celebration consisted of running a train on me, since I was the only girl that Red Roc had sent to service the party. By the time the fifth drunk nigga had taken his second turn at me, I couldn't do it anymore. My pussy was stretched and raw, my skin was bruised from the way they manhandled me, and my clothes were stained from the numerous times that some of the men had nutted on me.

While they smoked and snorted their way into oblivion I headed for the door, hoping that they were done with me for the night.

"Where you going, hoe!" One of them called out to me.

I turned around and plastered on a sexy smile. "To get more condoms, baby. You know mama gotta keep it fresh for you."

"While you out bring back some blunts. Don't take forever either, or I'ma have to tax Roc's ass and he ain't gon be too happy with you for dat."

"Be right back," I promised him as I opened the door and made my exit. Stupid fuck! I knew that they must have really been stoned out of their minds if they thought that I was coming back. It wasn't going to happen.

As I made my way to the elevator I felt my body staggering. I hadn't eaten anything all day and I was beginning to grow numb from the way my body had been repeatedly abused for the past three hours. Red Roc had gotten paid in advance for the party and I wasn't due to get my cut until after I returned to him. With the way I was feeling, I had no intentions of returning to the home where Red kept us girls. I now understood why Bambi had felt the need to hide out from him and rest her pussy as she'd stated when we met. I needed to do the same thing only I had no intentions of every returning to Red. There wasn't enough money in the world to prompt me to subject myself to that kind of torture any longer.

Standing in the elevator, I reached out to hold onto the wall. I was weak and didn't know how much longer I was going to be able to stay upright. I didn't even notice the man standing behind me and the way that he watched my every move. It wasn't until my body swayed backwards and he caught me just before I hit the floor that I noticed him. That night, that elevator ride, my eighteenth birthday was a momentous occasion that changed my life forever. It was the day that I met Reginald and the day that I reclaimed the power over my life.

***

Reginald was wealthy. He was a very affluent businessman with several Fortune 500 companies under his belt. He was one of the single leaders of a venture capital empire and the world was his oyster. He lived in a lavish penthouse apartment in Miami, which he'd whisked me away to after declaring that I needed a vacation. Somehow between our elevator ride and him taking me for coffee he'd determined that he could help me turn it all around. I don't know what made me open up to this complete stranger with whom I had nothing in common, but I had and once I did he began to lay the foundation for my future.

Reginald was single, he was in his late fifties, and he was dying. Some time ago he'd contracted AIDS from a woman he'd been madly in love with. He'd lived with the disease for nearly twenty years but his organs were beginning to fail as a result of it and he didn't have much longer on this Earth. He had no children, no one to take care of him, and no one who he dared to share the details of his personal hell with. He was in desperate need of a companion and someone to take care of him as he got sicker. His time was dwindling.

"When I saw you all wounded and helpless in that elevator you reminded me a

lot of myself," he told me. "A person in dire need of a helping hand and some compassion. A person in need of someone to put you before them if only for a moment."

I felt vulnerable listening to him pick me apart and tell me about myself. I didn't want to hear it and I damn sure didn't want to face the facts. I was broken. It was true. I needed a way to put me back together again.

"You lack confidence," he told me. "Without confidence you will always be a doormat. Here's what I'm going to do for you...I'm going to give you confidence."

I had to laugh. "I didn't realize that was the kind of thing you could just go around handing out."

"I'm a man with much wisdom and even more money," he stated. "Trust me, when I'm done with you there won't be

*another woman alive that can match your
confidence level."*

*I didn't know what to expect, but I
knew that nothing in life was free. "And in
return?" I was afraid that he was going to
want me to do what I did best at the time
and sleep with him. Remembering the way
my high school crush had ruined me with
gonorrhea, I had no interest in sleeping with
a man who'd just admitted to me that he had
AIDS.*

*"In exchange you'll stay with me. Be
my companion. Help me manage my affairs.
And when I'm gone, you'll be well
compensated."*

"Well compensated?"

*"Yes. Your time is valuable and you
are going to need funding to help you*

branch off into your new life once I'm gone."

I shuddered at the way he continued to prophesize his death. "Do you have to keep saying that?"

"It's the truth. And that's something else you'll learn from me. Not to sugar coat shit. Don't waste your breath on bullshit. Time is of the essence always."

"Will I have to sleep with you?" I came out and asked

Reginald smiled. "Getting right to the nitty gritty, huh? You catch on quick. No, I won't require sexual favors. I'm not trying to end your life. I'm trying to help you begin it."

And so it was. Reginald did exactly what he promised. He funded the cosmetic surgeries that transformed me into a vixen from facial reconstruction, to the breast implants, the butt injections, and even expensive hair fusion treatments. I looked like a totally different person by the time my body had healed and Reginald's money had been spent. He wasn't only concerned with my outward appearance, but he also wanted me to be in tune with who I was and deal with what I'd been through. Because of that he sent me to see a psychologist twice a week. In therapy we discussed how much I resented my mother and how much I resented my high school crush for being weak-minded enough to allow others to pressure him into making a fool out of me. Those two things fueled the anger that lived within me and I didn't know how I could ever forgive either of them for how they'd treated me.

Over time he realized that I although I'd come into my own and had developed into a true boss bitch personality, I still was unable to let go of that one part of my past. I'd reconstructed my body and mindset while preparing for the life I'd live without Reginald, but I wasn't healed from those two emotional wounds. Whenever the topic came up in conversation, Rodney could see the fury in my eyes. We'd spent several years together by that point and he knew me. He knew my heart.

"Sometimes, revenge can be freeing," he told me as he clicked away on one of his online Facebook support groups. "I'm not telling you go do anything in particular, I'm just telling you that I understand."

I sipped from a glass of Chardonnay as I looked over his shoulder at the conversation he was having. *"You wouldn't think less of me?"*

"I could never think less of you. You've taken great care of me. You've been loyal and I know that you're a loving person that's been scorned. Sometimes you have to do what you have to do in order to move on."

I was silent as I continued to read his conversation while considering how I would go about exacting revenge so that I could move on.

"What do you want to do?" He asked me, as if reading my thoughts.

"I want them to hurt the way I did," I whispered. *"I want them to feel the emotional distress that has sat with me all this time. I want them to know what it feels like to have your heart ripped in half."* A

tear found the corner of my right eye as I spoke. "I want it to burn the same way their actions stung me."

Reginald nodded. "Then you have to use the same tactics they used so they can feel what you felt. A person's emotions can really be dangerous."

His words spoke to me. In order to get back at my crush I needed to attack his reputation and then crush his heart, the same way he'd done me. But how could I do it?

"I'll get someone to find them," Reginald offered, again falling along my same mental wavelength. "We'll track them down, learn about their lives, and you can go from there. Formulate a plan, don't go in doing anything trivial or messy. I'll alert Darius that you may or may not need his

services. If anyone can help you with some less than legal activity and it not backfire then it's Darius."

Darius often worked as a body guard for Rodney when he had to go certain places or meet with certain people. I knew that Reginald's businesses had some illegal ties to them, but I never once questioned it. It wasn't for me to know. But I was smart enough to know that Darius' presence made it easier for Reginald to handle whatever under the table affairs he had going on. Darius was a very sexy, muscular brother who never once looked at me sideways. Although he knew that Rodney and I had an arrangement and were not intimate, he was still loyal to the man that cut him a check. I respected that although on occasion my loins ached for him. The fact of the matter was that I too respected Reginald and was loyal to him. During all of the years that I lived with that man, I never once slept with another guy although he granted me permission to do so discretely. To the outside world, Reginald's business associates, neighbors, and select friends, I was his woman. He didn't want anyone catching me with someone else and starting a scandal. To alleviate that and out of my undying loyalty to him, I simply became celibate.

When Reginald finally died in the middle of the night following a lavish dinner we'd attended for a local Dade County judge's retirement, I was crushed. It was as if my world had stopped. I'd lived for him, shared with him, and depended on him for years and now I found myself once again out in the world alone. But that time, my circumstances were different. Reginald was true to his word. After I arranged Reginald's memorial service and had him buried in the place of his choosing, I met with his attorney who informed me that Reginald had left me his home, controlling shares in two of his companies, and a hefty sum of 1.2 million dollars. I could barely breathe upon getting the information. The money would be issued to me over time, like stipends, via check or direct deposit once a month in order to make sure that I remained responsible with my new found wealth. Leave it to Reginald to want to keep teaching me things such as responsibility even in his death.

With my new look, my refined sense of self-worth, over the top self-confidence, and more money than I could ever use in my lifetime, I decided that it was time for me to use the information that Reginald's private investigator had pieced together for me. So, I visited a T-Mobile store and got a new cell phone with an Atlanta phone number, rented a condo via a short lease, and began to make a few phone calls. It was time for me to do exactly what he had told me it was okay to do: use the same tactics that they used so they could feel what I felt. The heat was about to be on in Atlanta. I could already see the blaze.

Chapter 13

Tyson

I had been waiting for Ari for a good twenty minutes before she finally made her way to the passenger side of my ride. It was a relief because I was so ready to get out of there. I couldn't believe that Lauryn had stolen my phone and actually sent photos of my dick to the women in my graduating class. How the hell did she even know about my class reunion or how to get the photos to them? I hoped the cops had finally caught up with her ass. First thing in the morning I was going to call and add defamation of character and stalking to her charges.

I pressed the button to unlock the door for Ari. I'd been sitting there with the doors locked just in case more husbands came at me about those damn pics. That shit was crazy. When Ari got in the car there was a strange look on her face.

"What's wrong?" I asked as I turned the key in the ignition.

"Nothing, just tired," she said in a low meek voice that I wasn't used to.

"A'ight, but are you sure that you're okay?" I was really concerned.

Part of me wondered if she was upset with me about those women having pictures of what was supposed to be for her eyes only.

"Yes," she simply stated.

"Baby, I didn't have anything to do with that. I think my ex stole my phone and…"

"But you told me that you left it at CVS Tyson. Why did you lie?" Her voice wasn't so quiet and meek anymore.

I shrugged my shoulders. "I didn't want to…baby…I didn't want to turn you off. I figured that if you thought Lauryn was out of control you wouldn't want to be with me."

"So you didn't think a liar is a turn off to me Ty?" She shook her head. "Just take me home. I've had it with you for one night."

I was appalled because nothing that had happened was my fault. She was right, lying was not a good idea and I should've just kept it one hundred with her.

"Babe, c'mon. Let me make it up to you. We didn't get to spend my birthday together, so let's not let the bullshit that happened tonight spoil our time now."

I didn't bring up what I thought had happened with Climaxx. At first I had braced myself for some type of backlash or a million questions about what had happened, but Ari hadn't said anything. That made me assume that what I thought had gone on was just a dream. Besides, I had woke up on the sofa fully dressed and Climaxx was long gone. Maybe I was just tired as hell, but I couldn't imagine falling asleep on a sexy woman while she danced for me.

Ari let out a loud sigh and then leaned back against the headrest. "I can't believe that happened. I'm sorry. I just...I don't take too well to my man misleading me. I've had enough of that in the past. See, I promised myself that I'd never allow another man to hurt me."

"And like I said before, I ain't perfect. I have a fucked up past, but I'm not trying to hurt you, Ari. Tonight was crazy. I wasn't expecting any of that shit either and—"

"What about the story your boy told me about that girl you fucked over in high school? Was that true?" That low, shy voice was back again. Ari didn't sound like herself at all.

I cleared my throat because I'd hoped she would forget about that. "It's not what you're thinking, babe. It wasn't that serious. We were all kids and so… shit happens."

"Really, shit just happens huh? You fucked some chick that you thought was beneath you as part of a bet and then just left her high and dry? Well, what makes you any different now than you were ten years ago, Ty?" She was looking straight ahead so I couldn't read her face at the moment. I had no clue if she was really as mad as she sounded.

"Let it go, Ari. I was in high school then. That shit is over and it has nothing to do with you!" I snapped.

She didn't say anything, but I could feel the tension. It was so thick that you could cut it with a knife.

"I'm sorry, baby." I reached out to touch her thigh, but she pushed my hand away. Were we having our first argument?

"Save it, Ty."

"Look babe, don't go home okay. Come with me and let me make it up to you. Please?" I brushed her hair away from her face and tried to make her look over at me, but she wouldn't. "Just say you'll come home with me."

"Okay," she finally agreed with a sigh. "But you have a lot of making up to do."

I was satisfied with that and my mind was on making her believe that I really did love her with all my heart. She was the woman that I wanted and I had hopes that I'd be redeemed for my past mistakes by doing right by her.

* * *

Once we were in the comfort of my home I ran a bubble bath and joined my woman in the huge garden tub. We sipped on wine and talked about anything other than that crazy class reunion. I was glad she didn't bring any of that shit up because I wanted to forget about it.

We'd made our way to the bed and my hands and lips were all over Ari's sexy body. I wanted her bad as hell because I hadn't had any of her good loving in a while.

"Hold up, baby…I wanna do something freaky." There was a smile on her face and that was all that she wore. Other than that she was butt naked and I was loving the view.

"What? I'm supposed to be making it up to you, not the other way around."

She winked at me and then walked over to my bureau to retrieve a few of my ties.

"Let me tie you up." Her eyes were sneaky, but I was feeling a little kinky too, so I gave in.

"As long as you promise to untie me," I teased.

She flashed a seductive smile as she made her way over to me. "I promise to do a whole lotta shit to your fine ass, so get ready for a night that you'll never…ever forget."

"Oh, dayum, lil' mama. You 'bout to put it on me huh?"

"You have no idea," she purred sensually as she used the ties to confine my hands and legs to the bed.

"You must've read Fifty Shades of Grey," I joked and she laughed.

"I did, but I didn't see the movie. Did you?" she asked playfully.

As a matter of fact I had gone to see the movie with my ex Crystal, but I remembered falling asleep on it. All I remembered was him tying old girl up with his tie.

"Nah, but my sister told me about it. Not really my cup of tea. Neither is this, but I promised I'd make it up to you. I guess you can get me to do just about anything right now to get in your good graces." I was starting to feel vulnerable because baby girl had tied me up real nice and tight.

As I pulled at my restraints to test them she continued to give me those sexy looks. I was turned on to the fullest.

"Bring it on, baby. What you gonna do?" I challenged her. "You gonna ride me or you gonna kiss me from head to toe."

"Hmm, you just wait and see, big daddy. I got some hot shit for you. If you think you're feeling the heat right now, you 'bout to feel an inferno." She fondled her breast and then actually licked her nipple.

"Oh fuck! That's what I'm talking about, Ari. Hell yeah, baby." In an attempt to loosen the ties on my hands I pulled, but they only seemed to get tighter.

"First, I want to tell you a little story." She sat down on the bed and softly kissed me on the neck.

"Okay lil' mama, if you wanna tell a story first do your thing. Just make sure that it's a sexy story."

Her warm, moist lips moved down to my collar bone. "Mmm... just listen, baby."

"Mmm, okay...damn...that feels good."

Ari started talking in a low, raspy voice that I wasn't used to. "Once upon a time there was a little girl who fell in love with a little boy when she was only seven years old. The only thing was he was popular and had a lot of friends. The girl however wasn't so outgoing and she only had one friend. As time went on her feelings for the boy grew. She was so in love with him that she would do anything for him, even give him her virginity. Her mother was a religious fanatic, so she felt guilty about her lustful feelings. She thought that she was tainted, but every time she saw him she knew that it was right."

I suddenly felt uncomfortable. Where was her story going? It was definitely not sexy, because I wasn't turned on at all.

"Uhh, baby…what does this story…"

"Shut the fuck up, Tyson!" She snapped. The look on her face was erratic and I'd never seen her look like that before. "You're going to listen to my story!"

"Okay, go ahead." Instantly I regretted letting her tie me up. Shit!

"She loved him more than life itself and when he finally asked her for her number, she was so happy. They talked on the phone almost every night for two months and she was so in love. She was so happy. Finally, her mother gave her permission to go out with her best friend, but she really planned to see him. They made love for the first time and it felt like nothing she could've ever imagined. He made her feel beautiful. When she got in her bed that night she dreamed of him and living happily ever after. Then she woke up the next morning and reality hit her in the face like a ton of bricks. She called him and he didn't answer. When she went to school the next day he ignored her and everybody laughed and pointed. She eventually found out that she was just part of a bet. A bet with his immature, small dick ass friends. The girl got pregnant and her mother threw her out. Not only that, but she found out that he had given her gonorrhea. She lost the baby and then learned that she'd never be able to have children again. Isn't that shit sad, Ty? Isn't that shit fucked up!"

I was stunned. Was she really that mad about that shit that she heard at the reunion that she had to make up a whole story about it?

"What the fuck, Ari?"

"Nigga, don't play dumb." She laughed wickedly and stood up. "It's amazing what a pretty face, nice teeth, fake tits and a fat ass can do to a nigga." When she shook her head and cocked it to the side she looked like somebody I once knew. That feeling had visited me several times before, but now I couldn't shake it.

What the fuck was she talking about? I was afraid to ask. With my legs and hands tied up, I didn't know what my girlfriend was going to do next.

"Look, babe. I was a seventeen year old boy then. I'm not the same person now…"

"You still don't get it, Ty? Look at me!" Tears fell from her eyes and I couldn't help but think that she had lost it.

What the fuck had happened?

"Baby, I'm looking at you. You're having a moment for some reason, but I can't do shit because you got me tied up. I thought we were gonna be doing something freaky, but this isn't what I had in mind."

She laughed, but it was short lived. Suddenly she had that crazed look on her face again. "I've been in love with you since the first time I saw you, Ty…"

"Uh, me too Ari, since the first day I saw you in that bank, baby."

"Hmm. Well, that's not the first time you saw me, Ty." She stared at me. "You don't know who I am yet? Was I *that* insignificant to you?"

I was perplexed because she just wasn't making any sense. "Ari…what—"

"Shit, fuck it. Let me make it clear to you! I've been following you for the past year. Not only by myself, but I hired a private investigator. I got the job at the bank because I knew where you banked at. I flirted with you on purpose. I set up the robbery because I knew that you'd be cocky enough to fall for that life is too short bullshit. I met your little boo Lauryn at a club a few months ago and it wasn't hard to get her on my team. Hmmm, old Ren. Did you know that she's locked up? All it took was for me to get all up in her business. When she mentioned you I told her that you were my ex and you had done me dirty too. If only she knew that I was the ugly, skinny girl with braces, no ass, no edges and a mother who was brainwashed by a cult. I know that you got ten points for fucking the religious virgin. You also had your senior fees paid along with your prom expenses. All at the cost of my heart, body and soul. Not only that, but you got me pregnant and just left me out there to handle all of those emotions alone. I really loved you, Ty. Shit, I really fucking loved you, but I was just a joke to you. Not only did you take away my chances of ever having a family, but you damaged me. You ruined me and now… I'm going to ruin you."

There was a sly, conniving smirk on her pretty face. Was she who I thought she was? It couldn't be. She looked nothing like her, but then again, some of her facial expressions reminded me of her. I wouldn't have ever thought.

"Oh shit…" Then I remembered that she'd tied my ass up to the bed. "I'm so sorry…"

She walked over to me with her cell phone in her hand. When she leaned over I was afraid of what she was going to do to me. Instead of pulling a gun from under the pillow like I expected, she played a video for me. My eyes focused on the small screen. There was Climaxx sitting on my lap. So, she'd recorded it.

"Mmm...Ty...damn..." Climaxx moaned. "You were right Ari, this dick is good."

When I looked closer I noticed that she was not just giving me a lap dance, but she was riding my dick raw style. How the hell? I was out of it and didn't remember that shit. Well, I remembered bits and pieces, but damn.

"I hate you, Tyson! I fucked you again only because I wanted you to be into me! I wanted you to finally want me and you did! I had your ass fucked up and that was all the fuck I wanted! Fuck you! I'm going to make you wish you were dead! I'm beautiful now and I hate that you made me feel so ugly! Guess who's gonna be ugly now, nigga!"

My heart started to thump in my chest, because I didn't know what she was going to do.

"I said I'm sorry! I never meant to hurt you back then! I never thought you were ugly! We were stupid teenagers and now we're adults. Why…how do you look so different?" Despite the situation I needed to know.

She looked nothing like herself. I had no clue that she was really Aretha Smith, the girl I'd impregnated in high school.

"Money can buy anything, but it can't buy a cure for what you got. Climaxx, well, that's her stage name. Her real name is Yasmin. She drugged you and fucked you that night. Yeah, I sent you a package alright." Ari smiled. "She has AIDS."

At first I didn't register what she'd just said. "She what?" I violently fought to get my hands free, but it was no use. "Untie me you crazy bitch!"

"Oh, I got one better for your ass!"

I felt something cold being poured on my body and face. I thought it was water until I smelled it. "What the fuck! Is that alcohol?"

Ari's laugh was wicked as it filled the bedroom. The turn of events was not what I'd expected at all. A nigga was scared. Karma was a bitch named Ari who was really named Aretha and she had come for my ass after ten years. I'd been cocky and I guess in some ways I deserved what she was dishing out to me.

"Don't kill me..." I whimpered. Was she really telling the truth about that stripper? "She really got AIDS?"

She didn't say a word. All she did was light a match before dropping it on the bed between my legs. The flames quickly danced closer to me and I fought hard to get free.

"Oh shit! Untie me! Fuck!" I tried my best to escape the heat from the fire, but it was no use.

All Ari, or Aretha did was laugh. The evil cackle made me shiver even as the hot embers licked my skin. Damn, I was literally on fire.

"Sometimes you just have to let it burn." She turned to walk away and I yelled after her frantically.

"Fuck! Untie me! Untie me, bitch!"

Epilogue

Ari

I didn't have a lot of time to waste. My plane was leaving in two hours and I needed time to get through the TSA checkpoint at Hartsfield International Airport. I knew the address I was heading to, because it hadn't changed in the last ten years. Driving through the neighborhood and pulling up to the small boxed house filled me with a sense of uneasy nostalgia. I had no real desire to relive the memories that wandered there, so I hurriedly exited the cab I'd taken over, tackled the two steps leading to the porch, and rapped on the front door.

It took her only a few minutes to open the door and when she did her facial expression was priceless. She opened her mouth to ask a question, most likely to inquire about who I was, but then shock stole her speech and she was unable to vocalize anything she was thinking. Her eyes said it all. I watched as she clutched her chest and studied me from head to toe. I got it; I was a sight to behold. But despite the many cosmetic changes I'd undergone one thing held true—a mother would always know her child.

"Aretha," she finally whispered as she leaned against the doorframe to brace herself. "My goodness…you came back. You're home."

"I'm not staying," I told her. "I only wanted to tie up some loose ends."

The night of Tyson's reunion I'd abruptly left the state, returning to my comfortable home in Miami. With my financial blessing I was able to hop a red eye flight right out of town. For over a month I laid low in my home, waiting for things to blow over in Atlanta. I kept tabs on the local news and knew all about how Tyson's neighbor Ms. Jennings had saved his life by calling 911 and getting the fire department to help him out as quickly as they could. From what I'd learned, Tyson hadn't given my name to the authorities, or if he had they weren't mentioning me as a suspect in the horrific homicide attempt.

During that month of waiting I'd hired a local crew to clean out my condo. I didn't need anything in it so everything went to charity. With my revenge played out I was beginning to feel a sense of relief and was ready to start over and build a real life for myself, possibly find love and find an inventive way to create a family. I needed to clear my head for a bit and enjoy the blessing and opportunity afforded to me courtesy of the only person who ever truly loved me: Rodney. But there was just one more thing that I had to settle before moving on. I couldn't start anew while holding on to that last piece of hurt.

"Come in," Mom insisted.

I shook my head. There was no way I was going to re-traumatize myself by stepping foot in that home. "For a while I've been keeping up with you," I told her. "When I first reached out to you I thought it was the right thing to do because of what I knew…what I'd learned."

Not only had Rodney's private investigator found out valuable information about Tyson for me, but he'd also found out what was going on with my mother. That information had given me conflicted feelings on how to deal with her. Now, I was no longer conflicted.

"When I needed you the most you turned your back on me," I reminded her. "You were so engrossed in falling in line with those people, those alleged religious folk, that you lost sight of what it was to be a good, decent person. To be a loving mother. Love is unconditional. Maybe you never learned that, but I know it to be true."

She shook her head. "That was so long ago…so, so long ago. So much has changed."

"I know it has. You know what else I know, Mom? I know that you're here struggling. I know that you're struggling with this ovarian cancer and that the people you thought would have your back the most are the very ones that have neglected you. The COGIC has done nothing for you. Bills behind, medical expenses piling up. I see the fragileness of your body…your spirit."

She looked down and took a deep breath. "All I prayed for…all I wanted was for my baby to come home."

"To take care of you?" I questioned. "The way you should have taken care of me?"

She looked at me with sorrowful eyes. "I'm sorry, Aretha. I really thought I was doing right by you. I did the only thing I knew to do."

"Which was shun me and toss me aside." I fought back the tears that were threatening to fall. "You have no idea the pain, hurt, desperation, and degradation I suffered from as a result of your lack of love and support." I sniffed. "But I didn't come here to unload all of that on you." I reached into my purse, pulled out a two thick manila envelopes, and handed them to her. "I came to bring you this. This is $10,000 in cash. It may not cover everything, but it'll give you some relief."

She held the thick packages in her arms and weakly looked at me. "Won't you come in and let's please talk. Baby, I—"

"I'm done," I stated flatly. "I've done more than I should have to help and now I'm done. You see, I wanted to show you how it felt to have your world turn on you…your own flesh and blood leave you helpless. But, karma's a bitch, Mom. And the universe worked that out without my interference because here you are dying and alone. This money…this is all I can do to help you and it's much more than you ever did for me."

I turned away without saying another word and dared not to look back at her as she whimpered out her apologies. It didn't matter. I'd made peace. The bible said to honor your mother and father and I'd given her the financial ability to handle most of her affairs. Aside from that, I had nothing more to give to her. Love had long since left me and now I was on my way to see about finding how to obtain that emotion once more despite all the hurt I'd endured. I climbed back into my taxi and avoided gazing out of the window as I rode away from my past.

***

The flight was nearly done with boarding and we were going to be pulling off soon. I kept glancing up to see if any more passengers were making their way onto the aircraft but no familiar faces greeted me. I looked down at my watch. Had he gotten my messages? Had he missed the flight time? Or was he just not going to show up? As the stewardess began to close the doors of the overhead compartments I realized that it was hopeless. Apparently, I'd be flying to Honduras alone. There was a cabana waiting there for me and would be my solitude for the next two weeks.

I placed my purse in the small space underneath the seat in front of me and nearly jumped out of my skin as a muscular shoulder brushed against my right arm.

"Did you know that they offer top shelf liquor during these first class trips?" He asked.

I stared at him in awe. Where'd he come from? How had I missed him when her boarded the plane? My facial expression must have amused him because for the first time in all the time that I'd known him I saw the man of steel crack a smile.

"What? You thought I wasn't coming?" He asked. "It isn't every day that the woman you've secretly lusted after for years sends you the offer of flying off with her to a remote location."

"You lusted for me?" My heart fluttered. I always knew that something was there between us, but hearing him confirm it made me feel real flutters that I hadn't experienced in a very long time.

Darius nodded. "Of course, but there's a time and place for everything."

"And this is our time?" I questioned, like a school girl needing guidance and reassurance.

He leaned forward and kissed my lips so gently that I wasn't really sure if the sentiment had really occurred or not. "This is our time," he stated.

A feeling stirred inside of me. A burning desire was building and I prayed like hell that this time I would get my happily ever after.

* * *

Tyson

The sound of the beeping machines made my mind drift off. I had no clue why it took me back in time. It was 2005 and I went against every principle that my parents had taught me. I'd started a war that I didn't know even existed until it was too damn late.

"Man, if you bag that bitch you'll get ten points. Ten points nigga! You gon' be a legend," Manny said with his eyes all wide as she studied the list of names on the roster in his notebook.

Since our freshman year we'd kept score on who we'd all slept with and had a point system that was set accordingly.

We were in the locker room after the first game of the basketball season. It was my senior year, so it was only right that I left an impression.

"Ten points?" I made the smirk face at him. "I don't give a fuck about no points. I'm gon' fuck Aretha man. It's no question. My only question is, what ya'll niggas gon' pay?"

Manny and my boy Curtis laughed. "A'ight, check this. We'll cover your senior fees, even prom," Curtis spoke up.

I slapped them both five. "Oh, it's on like popcorn. I'm gon' pop that cherry. Shit, ya'll know me. I'm that nigga. All the bitches want me."

Yeah, I sounded cocky, but in my heart, deep down, I knew that I was wrong. Aretha was actually cool and the more I got to know her, the less I wanted to make a fool of her. It was sad that her mother made her dress like that. When I really looked at her she wasn't bad looking. She was actually cute, but she had acne and was just not as developed as most of the chicks I knew. Even if she was nobody would know because her mother practically made her dress in burlap sacks every day.

I had to save face though. I couldn't show that I actually gave a fuck about a chick like her. She was definitely not on my level, well not according to my peers. When I walked toward my black Honda Accord after school that day, I heard a voice behind me.

"Ty!"

I turned around and noticed that it was Aretha. She had managed to pull herself together quite nicely. Something told me that she had changed when she got to school that morning. Her cute little skirt was unusually short and she even wore a tank top. The *outfit showed that her body was a lot sexier than I thought it was.*

Her hair was done all up and I wondered if her only friend Debbie had done it for her. Debbie wasn't the finest girl in school, but she was still a lot more fashionable than her best friend.

I smiled at her. "Aretha. What's up?" As I walked over to her her smiled widened.

"Not much. What you doin' later?" Her glossy lips looked inviting and I stared as she talked.

"Hopefully I'll be seein' you later."

With my smile, I attempted to warm her heart. It was obviously working.

"Hmm, well, I'm gonna be at Deb's later. I'll call you and we can meet up somewhere."

I nodded. "Cool. Uhh, I'm drivin' so I can scoop you."

"Well, that's even better. I'll talk to you later."

"Yeah, later."

Later that night she called me and I decided to pick her up a few houses down from Deb's so her mother wouldn't know what was going on. When I took her virginity, I really had no real intentions of hurting her, but I had to save face.

The next day in school Manny cornered me when I was at my locker.

"I heard you met up wit' ol' girl last night. You fucked huh?"

At first I didn't want to say anything about it, but then Curtis and a few more members of the basketball team walked up.

"We got you covered man," Curtis said pulling a wad of money from the pocket of his Guess jeans. "Shit, all of us went in. It's no way she gave up the twat. Her mama gon' give her an exorcism if she did. I don't even wanna think about what she and her cult gon' do to you."

They all broke out in laughter.

"Well, for your info, I busted that cherry. What the fuck did you think? I'm Tyson Reid nigga!"

They all pounded me up and I really felt like shit when Aretha walked past and they all just stared at her. She smiled at me and my heart dropped.

"Oh, hell, wait a minute. That bitch really likes you nigga! What, you ate the pussy too?" Manny asked.

I shook my head in disgust. "Hell nah man!"

My eyes followed Aretha down the hall. I didn't know that both of our lives would change forever that day. At that point I had no clue that Kristi had burned me when we had sex a week before. I never meant to give Aretha a STD. Shit, I never meant to ruin her life. It was all so stupid. For popularity in high school, I'd sold my soul and now I was paying for it.

"Ty, can you hear me?" A voice brought me back to the present.

My eyes slowly fluttered open and my ex-girlfriend Crystal's face came into focus. I'd been in ICU for a while in the burn unit at Emory, but I was slowly progressing. They had already informed me that I was HIV positive and had suffered second degree burns on my face and 75% of my body. If it wasn't for Mrs. Jennings I would've been dead.

I cleared my throat as my life played out in my mind. I'd been a fool and therefore I'd been repaid for my sins.

"Yes, I can hear you," I spoke up in a hoarse voice. I hadn't done too much talking lately.

Instead I'd decided to reflect on the mistakes that had led me to where I was at the moment. Lauryn was locked up, but I didn't feel any better. All that time she wasn't the real threat to me. She'd been Ari/Aretha's puppet for money to take care of her son. If only I'd played my cards right. If only I had just shown her and the women in my past some type of compassion.

There Crystal was, although I'd probably treated her the worst.

"Your parents just went to get something to eat. I'm glad to see you awake. You've been out of if for weeks," she said as she looked down at me with a solemn expression on her face.

I squeezed her hand which was enveloped in mine. "Don't look so sad. I'm gonna survive."

The thought of seeing what I looked like in the mirror made me shudder. I'd already made an attempt after they removed the bandages and I was traumatized. Damn, Karma had delivered a blow for my ass. Not only was I disfigured for life, but I was living with a deadly disease.

"I'm here for you Ty, regardless of what happened. I could never…no matter what…you don't deserve this."

Did I not? Although I was resentful about it, I thought I did. Yeah, I was young, but I knew what I was doing. I'd fucked up really bad and I was paying for it. Right when I was ready to change, BAM, my past had come back to haunt me. I wished I was dead, because the HIV infection complicated everything. Because of my compromised immune system I had to be in the hospital longer than I wanted to be.

"Thanks Crystal." That was all that I could say. I was tired and all I wanted to do was rest.

All I could do was remember how my charred skin felt as the flames engulfed my body. The pain was excruciating and I realized that it was only a fraction of what Aretha had gone through. The thought of her getting plastic surgery and plotting against me infuriated me, but what could I do. A woman scorned wasn't a woman to underestimate.

I'd reported Climaxx to the authorities for infecting me with HIV on purpose, but she was nowhere to be found. She no longer worked at Mardi Gras and so, I was at a dead end. Ari was long gone of course and I was crushed. Shit, I had really loved her, whether she was Aretha or not. I couldn't help but get teary eyed when I thought about it. It was really fucked up the way life had turned out for me.

"You're welcome, Ty." I felt her warm lips on my cheek and a tear formed in the corner of my eye.

"You think God'll forgive me?" I asked feeling the tears fall down the sensitive skin of my cheeks.

She sniffed. "Yes, just ask."

I closed my eyes and prayed. If Ari had taught me anything it was to be a man who treated others the way I wanted to be treated. Yeah, I wasn't the same. My skin was burned, I was dying and I was angry, but I was still a better man because of it.

The End

Other Titles by Author Nika Michelle

The Forbidden Fruit Series

The Black Butterfly Series

The Empress

The Love in the A Series

That "D" on the Side

Bout That Life: Diablo's Story

The Nookie Ain't Free

The Nookie Still Ain't Free

Other Titles by Author Kenni York

The Karma Series

The Girls

Over It

Ask No Questions

A Girl's Perspective: My Life in

Poetry

Sexcapades

The Twisted Love Series

Pink Slips

My Friend? My Foe?

Happily Ever After

Merrilittle: Murder in a Small

Town

CPSIA information can be obtained at www.ICGtesting.com
Printed in the USA
LVOW07s1835240116

471937LV00001BA/26/P